Knowing
GOD *as* FATHER

A Woman Learns to Trust in God's Care
BRIDGET PLASS

LOYOLAPRESS.

CHICAGO

LOYOLAPRESS.

3441 N. ASHLAND AVENUE
CHICAGO, ILLINOIS 60657

British edition 1996
North American edition 2001

Text copyright © 1996 Bridget Plass. Original edition published under the title *The Apple of His Eye* by The Bible Reading Fellowship, Oxford, England. Copyright © 1996 The Bible Reading Fellowship.

Unless otherwise stated, scripture quotations are taken from the Today's English Version—Second Edition. Copyright © 1992 by American Bible Society. Used by permission.

Scripture marked (NIV) is taken from the Holy Bible, New International Version®. Copyright © 1973, 1978, 1984 by International Bible Society. Used by permission of Zondervan Publishing House. All rights reserved. The "NIV" and "New International Version" trademarks are registered in the United States Patent and Trademark Office by International Bible Society. Use of either trademark requires the permission of International Bible Society.

Interior design by Eileen Wagner

Library of Congress Cataloging-in-Publication Data
Plass, Bridget.
    Knowing God as Father : a woman learns to trust in God's care / Bridget Plass.—North American ed.
        p. cm.
    Rev. ed. of: The apple of His eye. 1996.
    ISBN 0-8294-1608-0
        1. God—Fatherhood—Prayer-books and devotions—English. I. Plass, Bridget. Apple of His eye. II. Title.

BT153.F3 P53 2001
231'.1—dc21
                                              00-045418
                                            CIP

Printed in the United States of America
01 02 03 04 05 / 10 9 8 7 6 5 4 3 2 1

This book is dedicated with love to my mother and father, and also to Matt, Joe, David, and Katy, each one definitely the apple of my eye (whatever I may have called them at times!)

Contents

Section 3: Yes to Adventure

Section 4: Some Famous Last Words

Section 5: "God So Loved the World . . ."

Preface

I agreed to write *Knowing God as Father*—my first book—with
some trepidation, as I am neither a professional writer nor a biblical scholar. However, I have for years enjoyed communicating
the Bible through preaching and teaching, and more recently
through joining my husband Adrian in dramatic presentations
based on material from the many books he has had published in
the UK. As we travel farther and farther around the world, I am
often amazed that so many people in the church seem to have
missed out on the best truth of all, that they really, truly are
God's children and that he delights in them, not in some airy-
fairy sort of way, nor in an arm's-length, formal handshaking
sort of way, but in the extravagantly over-the-top way that we all
want to be loved by our parents and that, if we have them, our
children want to be loved by us.

As you read this book, I'd like you to join me in exploring
some aspects of this love, especially in the light of what Jesus
told us about his Father. We will be looking at some things that
took place during the last few weeks of Jesus' life here on earth
and at God's loving purpose in the lives of a few of his children.
I also hope you will join me in walking with Jesus himself as he
resolutely turns his face toward Jerusalem and his death.

This will be a very personal interpretation. My hope is that
through these reflections you will catch a glimpse of what it
means to know and trust God as father.   —BRIDGET PLASS

"Oh, and before I Go . . ."

You know how just before you go away you keep thinking of urgent messages that you want to leave behind? "Oh, and don't forget . . ." you keep saying to the people who will be staying at home or at work. You keep repeating this because your mind is so distracted and because every time you think of something it feels so vitally important that you just have to say it again.

Well, this is how it seems that Jesus felt during the period before he allowed himself to be taken to his death. But his urgent messages were not about groceries or the dry cleaners. They were all about God. "Did I tell you he's your Father? . . . Oh, and don't forget: he wants you to call him 'Father.' . . . You must remember he loves you like a father loves his child. . . . He loves you like I do. . . . When you've seen me, you've seen the Father. . . . Oh, and don't forget. . . ."

Do you know that John records the word *father* thirty-nine times in chapters 14 through 17 of his account of the last weeks of Jesus' life?

Because of Jesus' sense of urgency during this emotionally charged period, I thought we would begin these reflections by concentrating on a few of the startling facts about God our Father that his children have discovered throughout the Bible.

Refer Directly to Maker

You created every part of me;
*   You put me together in my mother's womb.*
I praise you because you are to be feared;
*   all you do is strange and wonderful.*
*   I know it with all my heart.*
When my bones were being formed,
*   carefully put together in my mother's womb,*
when I was growing there in secret,
*   you knew that I was there—*
*   you saw me before I was born.*
PSALM 139:13–16

Have you ever had the opportunity to see a photo of an ultrasound scan showing the human fetus at an early stage? I think it's one of the most marvelous things I have ever seen—a tiny knobbly lump holding all the intricate patterns of God's little masterpiece. Biology textbooks now all contain pictures of the developing embryo. My favorite is a photograph taken at eighteen weeks showing a minuscule thumb being sucked. Have you seen it? It is quite beautiful and seems full of mysteries. What color are those eyes, hooded at present by a delicate pink film? Is it a boy or a girl? Will it have big feet like Grandma, or Great Uncle's nose?

Having four children whose personalities are all quite individual, I'm particularly intrigued by another unknown quality. What personality will it have? Will she be a Martha or a Mary? Will he have a volcanic temper? What will make her laugh? How will he handle grief? What will be her thorn in the flesh? What will be his particular talent? God knows—literally! He knows every single thing about this being-to-be and, we are told, loves this child even more than any mother could.

I can't begin to explain why, even at this stage, some of these tiny miracles carry future pain within them, some physical or mental disablement that will make their lives so much more difficult than it is for most of us.

The only thing I can confidently pass on is something that a friend told me. Her name is Hilary McDowell, and she was born with a generous personality as well as multiple injuries to her minuscule body. With the determination, love, and faith of her family she was able to develop the first and overcome the second enough to lead a full life.

Hilary and I met at Carberry House, a Christian conference and holiday center in Scotland. In between her evening of performance poetry, her dance workshops for teenagers, and her counseling sessions as deaconess, we found lots of time to chat. She told me how sometimes it is very, very hard for her to get up in the morning. Looking forward to a day of painful physical struggle takes a daily dose of courage that occasionally deserts her at seven o'clock in the morning. On those occasions, she says she needs to look at the little poem she has stuck above the mirror in her bedroom. It is the shortest poem she has written and is included in her fascinating first book, *Some Day I'm Going to Fly*. The poem reads:

Any complaints about this model refer directly to maker!

That's it. A tiny statement containing the essence of the mystery of why we are as we are, as simple yet intricate as the embryo.

So many of us just don't like ourselves. We look in the mirror and we don't like what we see or what we know is inside. It is hampering our happiness, ruining our relationship with God, and turning up like the proverbial bad penny to prevent us from marching forward. So tell God about it. Tell him how you can't cope today, how fed up and unhappy you are. Take your complaints to him. He made you and he alone will be able to answer your questions. And, let's face it, he has loved you longest!

PRAYER

Dear Father,
Here I am, your child, your grown-up baby. Sometimes I don't like myself very much; sometimes I can't cope. Sometimes I want to give up. Sometimes getting up in the morning and facing the day is almost too hard to do. Sometimes I hate you for not sorting it out, for allowing the things that have made me who I am. Love me through it all, my dear Father, and help me to see myself as you see me. AMEN.

I'm Here, God

I call on you, O God, for you will answer me;
  give ear to me and hear my prayer.
Show the wonder of your great love,
  you who save by your right hand
    those who take refuge in you from their foes.
Keep me as the apple of your eye;
  hide me in the shadow of your wings
from the wicked who assail me,
  from my mortal enemies who surround me.
  PSALM 17:6–9 (NIV)

I had received a really depressed phone call from Adrian. He had been speaking for the first time in Germany, with the aid of a translator, and it had been very difficult. Although the tour had gone well and despite the tremendous hospitality, he had felt very lonely, as he spoke no German at all. He was longing to come home. So the children and I decided to surprise him by meeting his plane the next day.

Trying to give Adrian this sort of surprise is never easy—he is as notoriously disorganized as I am. It turned out that the arrival time he had given me was wrong by several hours. But of course we didn't know that, and having gotten up at the crack of dawn, we spent the better part of the day at Heathrow Airport with very little money and increasingly fraying tempers. In fact, by the time the monitor showed that his plane had landed, we were in a bad way!

Our two middle boys, having sparred all afternoon, had fallen out with a vengeance. The arrivals lounge at Heathrow hardly seemed a suitable venue for a shirt-ripping war, and I had become very cross with them both. Knowing how carried away I can get, I probably told them that they had not only let down their entire family but also their queen, their country, and indeed the whole human race. I don't recall exactly what I said, but I do remember the pall of shame that reduced them to a sad, snuffling huddle and my own feelings of failure.

I knew that they were feeling very bad about themselves, and I would not have been surprised if they had skulked at the back of the room when the words "baggage in hall" came up on the screen. It was therefore quite a surprise to me to watch them each choose a spot right in front of the crowd. Then Adrian came around the corner, and I watched his tired eyes light up when he saw his sons waiting for him. In that split second I learned something very important.

I meet so many Christians who are living their lives in a sort of "at-the-back skulk." Because they feel so ashamed of something they have done, they have convinced themselves that God would not particularly want to see them. I also frequently meet people whose sense of self-worth is so low that they find it difficult to pray, because they don't really think that God would want to hear from them.

Watching Adrian hugging his two grubby sons together, I knew. The reason why we, the inadequate ones, should feel confident enough to metaphorically stand at the front of the crowd and shout, "I'm here, God! Look over here, it's me!" is not because of what we are or how well we are behaving. It is quite simply because we are the apple of his eye. The sight of us can't help but give him joy—because he is crazy about us.

PRAYER

Dear Father,
Are we really that special to you? Can it really be true that what-
ever we may do, nothing can separate us from your love? Help us
to believe this. Help us to stand straight and tall and confident in
your love. Amen.

Heavenly Glue

This is the word that came to Jeremiah from the Lord: "Go down to the potter's house, and there I will give you my message." So I went down to the potter's house, and I saw him working at the wheel. But the pot he was shaping from the clay was marred in his hands; so the potter formed it into another pot, shaping it as seemed best to him.

Then the word of the Lord came to me: "O house of Israel, can I not do with you as this potter does?" declares the Lord. "Like clay in the hand of the potter, so are you in my hand, O house of Israel." JEREMIAH 18:1–6 (NIV)

One of our best local friends is a builder and decorator who also runs a small but lively church fellowship. This combination leads him to deal with very diverse situations, so we were somewhat intrigued when his small son solemnly announced one day, "I know what my dad does."

"Oh, do you? What does he do, then?" Adrian asked.

"He fills in cracks," Tom replied with considerable pride.

I had to work overtime to suppress my laughter. Knowing the wide variety of skills our friend needs to have to carry out his slightly unusual role, we felt his son had hardly done him justice. Fortunately, his dad also found it funny, his only worry being whether his son had been made to look silly when he told us.

This passage about the potter has caused me a lot of problems over the years. I have always had difficulty with the idea of being smashed and remolded, perhaps because I have felt so strongly that my pot is such a mess that starting over would be the only option for it! Consequently, I have wasted a lot of time trying to bash myself into shape on the sly, just in order to avoid the humiliation of God having to do it.

I have also had a fear that God wants us all to be exactly the same. This has caused me to panic on many occasions. The idea of a line of pretty, perfect, identical little pots in which I would somehow be the odd one out is a familiar one to me. Some church teaching has made me feel like that.

Three things have helped me greatly in my understanding of what the image of the potter means. They just might help you.

One is the above conversation between Adrian and Tom. The more I thought about it, the more I felt it was a remarkable parable of the way God has decided to be with us. He is the master potter, and each one of us is just a thimble of his creation. Yet our experience of him is of someone who is not offended by our limited understanding of how truly awesome he is. He can take it because he is huge and completely in control, not some temperamental prima donna who will hurl us to the wall because we have become dirty or misshapen through our contact with the world and have somehow let his image down. The problem is that the dirtier we get, the more distorted our image of him will be and the less likely we will be to trust him with the necessary repairs.

The second is the information that Jesus is continually trying to communicate to his followers about the fatherhood of God. Once we pay attention to what Jesus is saying, we realize that God is more likely—perhaps after quite a showdown—to lick the corner of a father-sized handkerchief and scrub off the grime once we have said sorry for any damage and filth we have deliberately inflicted on ourselves. Incidentally, Jesus also makes it clear that damage done to one of his new, unsullied pots by anyone else makes God very angry.

The third thing that has helped me greatly in understanding the image of the potter was hearing someone say that the potter never throws away the clay. When I heard that, I recognized that my deepest fear has been that I could be rejected completely by the master potter. Thrown away. Deemed beyond repair. I suspect I am not the first person to have felt like that.

Well, I felt such a surge of excitement and joy upon realizing the truth contained in that statement that I found myself wanting to perform one of those ludicrously extravagant punches in the air that accompany the scoring of a goal in football. Yes!

Of course! He's crazy about the clay. He chose it. He made us, every bit. He will never smash us to the point of nonidentity; he will only knead us into shape like an expert craftsman and clean us so that our intended individual coloring can be seen more clearly.

We haven't come off some assembly line supervised by bored workers longing for their next coffee break. Each one of us has been individually designed with passion and love and is intended to be unique. Every tiny chip that appears on the surface of our special glaze saddens our creator because his concern for us is that we should feel beautiful and useful.

But he's been using chipped pots to do useful things for him since the beginning of time. They're the only ones he has to work with—Isaac, Jacob, Moses, Gideon, David, Matthew, Peter, and Paul, to name just a few. Our creator always seems quite prepared to pour the heavenly glue of his love and support into any number of cracks if we, his children, are prepared to trust him.

Bearing all this in mind and wanting to impress you with my mature and balanced attitude toward my newfound confidence, all I can say is

I'm a little teapot,
short and stout.
Here is my handle,
here is my spout.
When I get all steamed up . . .

Well, perhaps not! I'll just go back to punching the air. Why don't you join me? Yes!

PRAYER

Here we are, Lord, a pile of chipped, grubby pots. We want to be useful again. We want to be beautiful in your eyes. Take us in your expert hands, dear Father, and do whatever needs doing in order for that to be so. We could all do with some heavenly glue! Thank you for loving us unconditionally. Thank you for making us exactly as you wanted us to be. Please forgive us for any damage we have done to ourselves and others and help us to be willing to begin the process of forgiving those who have deliberately violated us.

Here we are, Lord. Please begin mending us—however long it takes. **Amen.**

God Our Strength

When my thoughts were bitter
*   and my feelings were hurt,*
I was as stupid as an animal;
*   I did not understand you.*
Yet I always stay close to you,
*   and you hold me by the hand.*
You guide me with your instruction
*   and at the end you will receive me with honor.*
What else do I have in heaven but you?
*   Since I have you, what else could I want on earth?*
My mind and my body may grow weak,
*   but God is my strength;*
*   he is all I ever need.*
PSALM 73:21–26

$\backsim\!\!\circlearrowright$

I am about to tell you something about myself that won't impress you much. It's rather good about God, though. It was about a year after God had pulled my husband through a breakdown, stood him up, dusted him off, and given him a job to do. At first I had just been so thrilled to see Adrian regaining confidence, getting to know his spiritual Father, and proving to be rather effective in serving God and his people. It was particularly exciting to see how the books he was writing were having such a freeing effect on those who read them.

Gradually, however, I found that I was not actually feeling as happy as all that. Strong feelings of hurt and confusion began to dominate my life. I don't normally brim over with confidence, and I had been badly bashed by some of the side effects of Adrian's illness—the money worries, the insecurity, the isolation and loneliness—but through it all I had felt tremendous confidence that God would sort it out for us. Now he had, but there were new costs involved. I had thought that God would return our lives to how they had been before the crack-up. He hadn't.

It felt as though Adrian's life had begun at thirty-seven and three-quarters and our life together with all its recent intensity didn't exist. He had become overnight that most extraordinary phenomenon, a "famous Christian," and it seemed as though people considered him public property. He was frequently away from home, and I discovered that I was in fact very fed up with God and even jealous of Adrian.

"You don't actually care one hoot about me, do you?" I'd rage at God. "All you care about is Adrian. You just wanted to get Adrian well so he could work for you. What about me? Don't you care? Don't you love me at all?"

Looking back, I can see that a lot of that was a natural reaction to a long period of having to be strong, but at the time it was awful. Apart from all this ghastly hurt, I felt so guilty, especially when I began to take it out on Adrian. All day, when I knew he was going away, I'd really try to be a good Christian wife—and then just as he was going out the door my good resolve would disintegrate and I'd hear myself yelling like the proverbial fishwife. Poor Adrian frequently had to stand in front of hundreds of people telling them how much God loved them and wanted to set them free—with my cruel words ringing in his ears. At last, I decided that I must do something or I would destroy all the healing that had taken place in my husband and endanger the work God had given him to do. I decided to get away for a few days to sort out my life.

I traveled to Scargill House in Yorkshire, armed with questions and arguments to put to God, and I think I fully intended to return home having decided on some sort of job that would fulfill me and make me mind less about Adrian's new lifestyle.

When I got there, an extraordinary thing happened. It was as though suddenly I could see clearly again after a long period of blindness. Absolutely no insights about my life came to me. My problems seemed quite irrelevant. All I could think about was Jesus. It was as if he held me by the hand for the whole of the three days I spent there. I experienced the kind of senseless joy that you only experience when you first fall in love.

Of course there were practical areas of our lives that we still had to sort out. But at least I knew that I was going to be able to look at them realistically and face the fact that our lives would never be as they had been before, because I had been reminded that God is my strength and that he will be to me all that I need.

PRAYER

Dear Father,
Sometimes we can end up so far away from you, blinded by our anger, stupefied by our hurt. If we have grown confused, take control of our lives, we beg you, Father. If we have become lost, come find us and bring us home. We miss you. We want to see you again. Come soon. AMEN.

Wide, Long, High, and Deep

[I pray] that Christ may dwell in your hearts through faith. And I pray that you, being rooted and established in love, may have power, together with all the saints, to grasp how wide and long and high and deep is the love of Christ, and to know this love that surpasses knowledge—that you may be filled to the measure of all the fullness of God.

Now to him who is able to do immeasurably more than all we ask or imagine, according to his power that is at work within us, to him be glory in the church and in Christ Jesus throughout all generations, for ever and ever! Amen.

EPHESIANS 3:17–21 (NIV)

I was still in Scargill and the last day of my miniretreat had arrived. I woke early to the strange sound of nothingness, and peering through the misted window I realized that it had been snowing heavily during the night.

As stunningly lovely as the countryside looked, I was worried. How would we all get out? The conference center was surrounded by tiny lanes that would already be inches deep in snow. I hurried downstairs and found several people already packed and preparing to go. "I've just been listening to the local news," one of the leaders announced. "The forecast for later on in the day is pretty dire, but the local roads are still passable. So it's really a choice of going now or preparing to be snowed in up here for a few days."

If the whole family had been with me I think I would have decided to stay. Snowballing and sledding with them in the Yorkshire Fells would have been heavenly. But they weren't. They were three hundred miles away in Hailsham, and I was missing them like mad. I ran upstairs, grabbed my bag, and hurried downstairs to hug and thank and skid my way to the car.

The first twenty miles were nasty, but eventually I made it to the highway. Relaxing, I turned on the car radio. The news was worse than I'd thought possible. Apparently, roads all across the country were in chaos. Accidents were becoming commonplace and people were being firmly advised not to venture out unless their journey was absolutely vital. Conditions seemed to be getting more treacherous every minute.

The snow was coming down thickly, and visibility was getting worse. So was the news, which included reports on crashes and breakdowns, warnings to stay in the car at all costs, and advice not to venture out without a defroster, thermos, and flashlight. I had none of these things and was very aware that I had been silly to attempt the journey.

All the euphoria that I had experienced over the last few days was gone and I felt frightened and incredibly vulnerable. So much for my renewed closeness with God. So much for feeling that he really did care deeply about me after all. Visibility became even worse as tears began to pour down my face. I was two hundred miles from home, freezing cold, and it was beginning to get dark.

At that moment, my car gave a groan and shuddered almost to a halt. I was aware of someone swerving to avoid me. Now I was slithering along at two miles an hour, sure that at any minute I would be hit. In front of me, I could just make out a sign indicating a turn to the left. Deciding that anything would be better than breaking down on the highway, I wobbled the car onto the side road. I could see nothing. "My lights must have gone out," I thought, and immediately, with a horrifying bang, the car stopped completely.

I sat there in the pitch darkness in my dead car and cried out to God in desperation. Then I opened my eyes. There to the left of me, its blurry lights just visible through the driving snow, was a café and a travel lodge.

Now, I have heard of people who believe that God runs ahead of them every time they go to the supermarket just to reserve a parking space for them—and quite honestly I don't have a lot of time for the idea that Christians should expect continual privileges. But I do believe that on that night God arranged exactly when and where my car would break down. Later that night, having phoned home and my travel club, I sat warm and safe in bed with a cup of tea, watching horrendous television news pictures of abandoned cars on motorways up and down the country.

I will never forget the sense I had of my heavenly Father being very close to me and saying, "I had to prove to you somehow how wide, long, high, and deep my love is for you, you stubborn woman!"

I wonder how he'll show you.

PRAYER

Dear Father,
We so want to feel close to you. Help us to open ourselves to the possibility that you will meet us and that you really do want us to experience the depth of love that Paul is talking about here.
AMEN.

Break Out the Smarties!

Lord, you have examined me and you know me.
You know everything I do;
>*from far away you understand all my thoughts.*
You see me, whether I am working or resting;
>*you know all my actions.*
Even before I speak,
>*you already know what I will say.*
You are all around me on every side;
>*you protect me with your power.*
Your knowledge of me is too deep;
>*it is beyond my understanding.*
PSALM 139:1–6

The tremendous good news contained in this psalm was highlighted for me by something that happened yesterday. I was at a club that the churches in our town jointly hold for local children, many of whom come from difficult backgrounds.

It had been an exhausting but exciting morning, and I had been particularly pleased with the behavior of one small tough guy. When he had started coming to the club, he had been impossible to reach and had reacted aggressively to just about everything. Gradually, over a period of about two years, his suspicions had eased to the point that he even allowed a little teasing and physical contact. On this day he had been lovely, and I wanted to show him how pleased I was.

"Patrick, I'm really proud of you. Here's a special secret prize for trying so hard," I whispered, surreptitiously opening the "prize box" and sliding a tube of Smarties into his hand.

"Fanks, Miss," he said, beaming, and ran off, shoveling handfuls of sweets into his mouth as he went. I put the lid back on the box, placed it on the table, and went off to help with the straightening up, replacing of felt-tip pen lids, and scraping of glue off tables that inevitably accompanied the close of these meetings. I felt very happy.

Ten minutes later my friend Phillippa put something into my hand. It was an unopened tube of Smarties.

"I saw Patrick pinch it from the prize box on the way out," she said, smiling, "so I thought I'd better tackle him."

"Oh no," I groaned, "and I'd only just given him exactly the same thing as a prize for being so good today!"

"Well," she laughed, "look at it this way. Six months ago he would have denied he took them and probably kicked me in the shins for insulting him!"

God knows exactly where we all start our Christian walk. He knows our weaknesses and exactly why we are as we are, and it could well be that all of heaven rejoiced that morning because Phillippa didn't have her shins kicked.

It's easy to see God's loving forgiveness and encouragement with regard to little Patrick. But how about yourself? I wonder what we may have done recently that has made heaven rejoice? What small step have we made toward depending more on God? What temptation have we resisted? What kind thought have we had? It may not seem like much to us—and I know my own progress seems agonizingly slow—but to a God who knows us inside out it may have brought a smile and even heaven's equivalent to a hug and a tube of Smarties.

PRAYER

Dear Father,
Thank heavens you know everything about us. You see exactly
where we began, what the obstacles are to our progress, and exactly
where you would expect us to be right now. Give us strength to
pick ourselves up when we fail and to carry on, knowing that you
will be so pleased to see every little step of progress in our stum-
bling walk toward you. AMEN.

Whose Side Is God On?

Once again the Lord spoke to Jonah. He said, "Go to Nineveh, that great city, and proclaim to the people the message I have given you." So Jonah obeyed the Lord and went to Nineveh, a city so large that it took three days to walk through it. Jonah started through the city, and after walking a whole day, he proclaimed, "In forty days Nineveh will be destroyed!"

The people of Nineveh believed God's message. So they decided that everyone should fast, and all the people, from the greatest to the least, put on sackcloth to show that they had repented....

God saw what they did; he saw that they had given up their wicked behavior. So he changed his mind and did not punish them as he had said he would.

Jonah was very unhappy about this and became angry. So he prayed, "Lord, didn't I say before I left home that this is just what you would do? That's why I did my best to run away to Spain! I knew that you are a loving and merciful God, always patient, always kind, and always ready to change your mind and not punish." JONAH 3:1-5, 10; 4:1-2

✎

*T*his story of Jonah contains some wonderful news, not that if we choose to disobey God he might arrange for us to be swallowed by a very large fish, but that God cares deeply for each one of us and will forgive us—the recorded reason for Jonah's disobedience. Jonah didn't want to tell the citizens of Nineveh that God was angry about their behavior because he knew without a doubt that if they said they were sorry God would forgive them.

Jonah knew God. He saw God's readiness to forgive as an infuriating weakness until God pointed out to him, through the picture of the vine, that the reason he would try again and again to give the people of Nineveh a chance to repent was that he had watched them grow up and cared deeply for each one of them.

Several years ago I came across an example of the same unequivocal sureness about what God would do. Adrian and I have a friend who grew up in a series of foster homes and became increasingly disturbed by the process. At eighteen she was dumped into bed-and-breakfast land, armed with tranquilizers and a severe lack of self-confidence, to fend for herself.

At that stage in her life she was in a terrible mess and had entered into a series of unhappy relationships. She knew we worried about her and she phoned frequently to keep us posted about her struggles. At one point, she was living with a man who had left his wife, and we knew she was hoping against hope that this time the relationship would lead to marriage.

Late one night, she phoned to tell us, amid many tears, that he was thinking of going back to his wife. Of course, we both felt acutely sorry for her, and I finished our long chat by saying, "Before I go to bed I'll pray for you both."

"Uh, don't do that, Bridget" came the scandalized reply. "You know whose side he'll be on!"

Her instinctive response revealed more faith and confidence in the reality and righteousness of God than many sermons I have heard before or since. She and Jonah had a lot in common. Neither wanted God to intervene because they were sure they knew whose side he would be on.

Do I have that confidence? I find that as I grow older I am less sure than I used to be about exactly how I think God will behave in specific situations, but increasingly confident that whatever he does will be right. In fact, the more I get to know just a fraction of his heart, the more I feel able to agree with what Dame Julian of Norwich said: "All will be well and all manner of things will be well."

PRAYER

Dear Father,
Thank you for the story of Jonah. What mind-blowing stuff! We want to get to know you like Jonah did. We want to trust deep inside that you will always do what is just and fair. Help us.
AMEN.

The Offer of Safety

This is what the Lord Almighty says: "Once again men and women of ripe old age will sit in the streets of Jerusalem, each with cane in hand because of his age. The city streets will be filled with boys and girls playing there."
ZECHARIAH 8:4–5 (NIV)

⌒ᗐ

$\mathcal{W}$hen I came across these verses recently, I felt as if I had found an answer to something that has been troubling me for a very long time. Why don't we feel the same urgency that Jesus felt to tell the world about God? Of course, some of the reasons are obvious—laziness, fear, indifference—but I think one of the most crucial reasons is that deep down we don't think our world will want anything that God has to offer. We think our message is too unworldly for our world.

When Adrian and I went to Australia for the first time, we attended a marvelous conference organized by the Uniting Church. They had chosen for their title "This Is the Life," and I remember being told on the day we arrived the reason for their choice. It was explained that Australians would only be attracted by a positive lifestyle message because of the deep-seated self-made philosophy that had served them so well. The gospel, with its message of self-sacrifice, was apparently not much of a winner here.

When we returned two years later and got to meet Australians from more parts of the country, we appreciated the reasons for their choice. But we also realized that on a deeper level, many of them were desperate to be allowed to be vulnerable and to admit their feelings of fear and insecurity. More tears were shed during that tour than on any other, and many of those tears were shed by men who were discovering that what God was offering them was what they had always really wanted.

For me, that was the key to understanding what God had said to Zechariah, because I realized that what God wants for us is what we—and I mean the whole world—most want for ourselves: security, a world where our old people and our children can walk and play safely in our streets.

I was standing in our local children's playground watching with pretend gasps of horror as my friend's small boy attempted to swing hand over hand along the high, brightly colored monkey bars. "At least he can't hurt himself," I whispered. "This new surface is brilliant; he'll practically bounce." I turned to call my four-year-old daughter Katy to come off the slide and have a try. But no one was on the slide. Or the swings. Or the merry-go-round. Three small boys occupied the wooden pirate ship, shouting bloodcurdling threats of plank walking for invaders, so I knew she couldn't be there.

Panic doesn't set in slowly. It rushes in and engulfs like a monstrous wave. I began to run around the small fenced-in area, willing her to be tucked behind the wooden bench or under the slide. The specter all parents fear was filling my mind.

Then I saw her dancing and jumping across the recreation field with her hand tucked securely into that of her big brother. She had seen him coming and had run to meet him. Nothing to worry about this time—but as I stood there watching her, a stark truth hit me. Technology has at last created safe surfaces on which young children can play, but no caring parents will let their small children out of their sight to play on them. The danger is too great.

Maybe this is a clue as to how to speak more confidently to those who don't want to hear. So very often we hear God described by those who haven't met him as a demanding tyrant or an indifferent judge. Yet he is acknowledging as vitally important the very thing we all yearn for most.

PRAYER

Dear Father,
Give us the confidence to tell our world about you. Help us to
remember that you care deeply about your world and want safety
and peace for every one of your children, young and old. We want
to apologize for all the times we have missed opportunities to talk
about you or have misrepresented you in some way and so not
given strength to your word. Lastly, Father, as your children, we
ask you to please keep our loved ones safe. Amen.

Back to Eden?

*Then God said, "And now we will make human beings; they
will be like us and resemble us. They will have power over the
fish, the birds, and all animals, domestic and wild, large and
small." So God created human beings, making them to be like
himself. He created them male and female, blessed them, and
said, "Have many children, so that your descendants will live
all over the earth and bring it under their control. I am putting
you in charge of the fish, the birds, and all the wild animals. I
have provided all kinds of grain and all kinds of fruit for you
to eat; but for all the wild animals and for all the birds I have
provided grass and leafy plants for food"—and it was done.
God looked at everything he had made, and he was very
pleased.* GENESIS 1:26–31

❧

Adrian and I spent the summer of 1995 working in South
Africa. It was a tremendous experience for all of us, and we met
some fascinating people.

Yuri and his wife, Pippa, ran a small safari lodge on the edge
of Kruger National Park. At the end of our speaking tour, we
spent three of the most exciting days of our lives there.

None of us will forget the smells and sights of our early
morning treks into the bushveld, bumping along excitedly in an
open-topped jeep. We saw many wild creatures, sometimes from
a quite frighteningly short distance.

One of our most memorable experiences, however, didn't involve elephants or lions. It was a walk along a quiet trail through the area of wilderness right next to the camp. We were with Yuri, a trained ecologist, and Dixon, our South African ranger, who followed closely with a loaded rifle, just in case. Yuri was a veritable mine of local knowledge, continually throwing out nuggets of information as we walked. We learned more in that hour as we strolled along looking at bushes and insects than I would have imagined possible.

There was the baobab tree, which has fireproof bark to protect it from the fires that burn the savannah to the ground every year during the hot dry season and provide fertile soil for renewed growth. There were the follow-the-leader troops of ants; a discarded tortoise shell whose pattern revealed the age of its former owner, long dead; twigs that had traditionally been used as toothbrushes; and, from another bush, leaves that were once the only available toilet paper.

We saw termite heaps that, after falling into disuse, become desirable residences for the dwarf mongoose, and we caught tantalizing glimpses of vervet monkeys foraging for berries. Most moving of all were the little piles of bones that denoted the burial sites of the indigenous tribes that had lived there until the scourge of apartheid had forced them to leave. We were walking in what is thought to be the cradle of humanity, and on that sun-drenched morning it felt like Eden.

This feeling was fueled by something that Yuri had told us. Apparently the ecosystem of this area belies the theory that humans are superfluous to the natural world. Anyone who has seen or read *The Jungle Book* knows that the king of the jungle needed a human—Mowgli, the man-cub—to teach the animals the secret of how to make fire. The savannah has always needed fire in order to prevent excessive bush encroachment and to maintain lush and palatable grass for the many herbivores that provide food for the carnivores, and so on along the food chain. Humans provided the knowledge the savannah needed for survival.

Much of what Yuri had said was way over my head, but I felt that we were privy to a very special understanding of the creation story, made even more poignant by his references to a tiny bird called the honeyguide bird, whose sole function throughout living memory has been to tell people where honey can be found. The bird sits in a tree and calls until a human being hears it. Calling constantly and flitting from tree to tree, the bird guides its followers, sometimes for several days, to a place where a hive full of honey awaits them. Once the human being takes the honey, the bird eats the wax and the bee larvae.

It is easy to see how important this bird's role must have been in the days when honey might have been people's only source of sweetness. Now the bird is redundant. The people who belong here have been driven from their territory into the inappropriately named "homelands," and even though more than a year has passed since the democratic elections, it seems unlikely that they will be able to return. The only occupants of the area are tourists and safari-camp owners, who are far too busy to spend several days seeking sweetness that they can buy in the local supermarket. Now the honeyguide bird faces extinction.

This profoundly sad story seems to offer an insight into the even greater tragedy of human sinfulness. Almost as old as the world itself, the "sin chain," the inevitable consequence of greed, selfishness, and lust for power, has again and again disregarded and destroyed the delicate balance that is always supposed to exist between people, God, and the natural world.

PRAYER

Dear Father,
We know we can't turn back the clock to the time when everything
in your beautiful world was in harmony. All we can do is ask for-
giveness for the way we have treated our part of it. Help us to
understand how we can best improve our corner of the universe
and give us courage to stand against those who are trying to
further destroy the balance. AMEN.

Our Father . . .

You are all sons of God through faith in Christ Jesus, for all of you who were baptized into Christ have clothed yourselves with Christ. There is neither Jew nor Greek, slave nor free, male nor female, for you are all one in Christ Jesus. If you belong to Christ, then you are Abraham's seed, and heirs according to the promise.

What I am saying is that as long as the heir is a child, he is no different from a slave, although he owns the whole estate. He is subject to guardians and trustees until the time set by his father. So also, when we were children, we were in slavery under the basic principles of the world. But when the time had fully come, God sent his Son, born of a woman, born under law, to redeem those under law, that we might receive the full rights of sons. Because you are sons, God sent the Spirit of his Son into our hearts, the Spirit who calls out, "Abba, Father." So you are no longer a slave, but a son; and since you are a son, God has made you also an heir. GALATIANS 3:26—4:7 (NIV)

⟳

*H*aving just returned from our last tour, I realize that one of the characteristics of traveling is that you both lose and acquire things. A pile of underwear left in a hotel drawer, a sweatshirt on a boat, a handbag stolen, while the whole of the Southern Hemisphere must be littered to the point of ecological disaster with Plass combs and odd socks! Yet our bags get ever heavier. We return home with innumerable mini-shampoos and bath gels; a wonderful gift painstakingly woven by a group of ladies in Queensland; a special bottle of wine from the Barossa Valley; a plethora of miniature koalas and kangaroos and keyrings for presents; a hotel towel that was mistakenly dyed pink in the guest laundry—the list seems endless.

Other more interesting things that were acquired along the way helped make the heavy case easier to carry. Friendships struck up, sometimes over periods of only twenty-four hours, delve deeper into our hearts than those that we have had for years. Enthusiasts communicated their involvement with such commitment and joy that their causes were irresistible, as was the case with one of our tour sponsors, World Vision.

Aside from all of this we have acquired a truth that will never leave us, a knowledge of how truly tiny and vulnerable we all are, of how much God must love and care for us. That may sound trite, but everywhere we go we meet people who are struggling with their relationships, health, and work; people clinging to each other to prevent themselves from being blown over by the tornado of life; people who love and need love; people who worry; people whose hard shell of success has been cracked by God so that his love can flow in; people who have never even developed a shell. Children. All children. One huge, loving, squabbling, diverse crowd of kids who don't understand that they don't need to prove anything to be right, first, taller or greater, cleverer or more talented, because God has fathered us all and, in a way we'll never understand, can hold us all, wipe away our tears, and listen to all our adventures. Our Father, Abba, who art in heaven, hallowed be thy name.

PRAYER

Dear Father,
It is so easy for us to look at the differences between us, your chil-
dren, in a critical way. Help us to understand, just a tiny bit, the
mystery of your ability to love all of us with such passion that you
gave your Son to die for us. Help us to stop squabbling, to share
what we have, and to enjoy each other's special gifts without feel-
ing jealous. Above all, help us to learn from one another so that
our understanding of your greatness can also grow.   AMEN.

Too Busy?

"This is the message from the Amen, the faithful and true witness, who is the origin of all that God has created. I know what you have done; I know that you are neither cold nor hot. How I wish you were either one or the other! But because you are lukewarm, neither hot nor cold, I am going to spit you out of my mouth! You say, 'I am rich and well off; I have all I need.' But you do not know how miserable and pitiful you are! You are poor, naked, and blind. I advise you, then, to buy gold from me, pure gold, in order to be rich. Buy also white clothing to dress yourself and cover up your shameful nakedness. Buy also some ointment to put on your eyes, so that you may see. I rebuke and punish all whom I love. Be in earnest, then, and turn from your sins. Listen! I stand at the door and knock; if any hear my voice and open the door, I will come into their house and eat with them, and they will eat with me."

REVELATION 3:14–20

⁓◯

*F*or years, I envied some friends of ours whom we met shortly after Adrian and I were married. We were very hard off and they seemed by contrast to have a tremendous lifestyle. They had money and a beautiful house. Complimentary tickets to Ascot, London theaters, and Lord's, first-class travel, and a sumptuous car were just some of the perks that went with the husband's job.

Then one day he was laid off, just like that. Money was not a problem at first; a generous severance package saw to that. But there would be some grave fallout from the bomb that had hit them. Some of the effects were immediate, such as the repossession of the company car. More bruises appeared over the next few weeks. Sleeplessness, fear for the future, anger, tears of inadequacy, and the inevitable questioning as to where he had gone wrong. All this was ghastly to see, but the worst wound had yet to surface.

A few months after her husband had lost his job, my friend came to see me in a terrible state. "Our marriage is over," she sobbed. "We've been together nonstop since he was laid off, and we've found we don't know each other at all anymore and we certainly don't love each other."

"But this is all such a shock for you both and you're both going through so much, I'm sure you'll be okay. . . ." I fumbled on and on.

"You don't understand. We've not been close for years and we've both known it really but we've opted for a fun way of life and filled our lives so full that it hasn't worried us too much. He went to work at six A.M. and didn't get home till eight, and on Sundays he played golf, so we only had to get on for one day a week at the most and usually we had an invitation to dinner or tickets to a show. So we haven't had to work at it at all. And it's all gone. The love? It must have crept out years ago. We never even saw it go—and now that we need it, it's not here."

It was so sad and so final. It reminded me of a poem I had asked Adrian to write for me to perform years ago.

PHONE CALL

(Phone rings. Picks it up.)
Oh, Jesus? Don't come round tonight.
I'm busy at the hall
So chances of a chat with you are really rather small.

Well, so many people need me and I can't deny them all.
So . . . Looks as if I won't be in if you decide to call.
Tuesday? Would be better,
But I think the man next door
Is looking rather troubled . . . well I've helped him out before.
Friend in need, something you can never quite ignore.
So, don't come round tomorrow night, you'll understand I'm
sure.
Wednesday's our study night, Thursday I'm away.
Friday? I've got tickets for the local Christian play.
Saturday's the mission and that'll take all day.
No, better that we leave it now till Sunday night, OK?
(Almost replaces receiver. Suddenly snatches it back to ear.)
Oh Jesus? . . . Do you love me?
Will you ever set me free?
I've built myself a prison.
I've thrown away the key.
I'm weeping in the darkness, Lord.
I'm longing now to see the plans you have for both of us.
Please come and visit me.

Let's face it. All our relationships need working on, and if we don't work on them they can become lukewarm, especially our relationship with God. We can be so busy enjoying the worship, the speakers, the social life, the meetings (even criticizing the leaders)—the whole caboodle that we call church—that we end up, without realizing it, feeling that we have all we need and forgetting completely about our personal relationship with our Father.

But if we are not spending time with him, expressing our needs, involving him in our stresses, crying all over him with joy and thanks, and even grumbling at him sometimes, then this sort of blind feeling of self-sufficiency is inevitable. The greatest danger lies in the fact that the farther away from him we get, the less we feel we need him, the less we understand him, and the less likely we are to want to sort out our relationship with him. If that happens, we may well find that we have built ourselves a prison and have thrown away the key.

There is always hope. Our friends' marriage didn't recover— but then one of the partners in it wasn't God. Just look at the amazing message communicated to us from the risen Lord Jesus through one of his closest friends left here on earth. He may be pretty fed up with the church in Laodicea, but here he is, offering to supply everything necessary to repair the broken relationship. As soon as we become concerned about the distance that has opened up between God and us and turn to him in earnest, he is there for us. He will never force open the door, but if we invite him to come in, he will. He will sit down and eat with us and we will eat with him. Nothing will have changed at all.

⟡

PRAYER

Dear Father,
Please don't let us get so far away from you that our love grows cold. Hold us tight. Never let us go. We bring all our relationships to you now. We ask for your help and advice in those areas where things have gone wrong. Thank you for always being consistent in your love for us. Please come and visit us today. We'll try to have the door open for you. AMEN.

Beware, Bloodsuckers!

When his father-in-law saw all that Moses was doing for the people, he said, "What is this you are doing for the people? Why do you alone sit as judge, while all these people stand around you from morning till evening?"

Moses answered him, "Because the people come to me to seek God's will. Whenever they have a dispute, it is brought to me, and I decide between the parties and inform them of God's decrees and laws."

Moses' father-in-law replied, "What you are doing is not good. You and these people who come to you will only wear yourselves out. The work is too heavy for you; you cannot handle it alone. Listen now to me and I will give you some advice, and may God be with you. . . ."

Moses listened to his father-in-law and did everything he said. He chose capable men from all Israel and made them leaders of the people, officials over thousands, hundreds, fifties and tens. They served as judges for the people at all times. The difficult cases they brought to Moses, but the simple ones they decided themselves.

Then Moses sent his father-in-law on his way.

EXODUS 18:14–19, 24–27 (NIV)

◦⟋

*W*hen I was writing about some of the things that Yuri told us during our memorable walk through the South African bush, I remembered another amazing story that at the time both Adrian and I felt was an all too apt parable of one of the ways in which we become exhausted and drained of energy. Our attention was drawn to a bush, which I remember as being about the height of a person, with lots of pretty silver leaves.

"This is called the silver-leafed terminalia," Yuri informed us. "Can you see anything unusual about it?"

We peered at it hopefully, like children on a school trip examining relics in a museum, and willed an intelligent answer to surface. All I could see was a bush whose beauty was marred by an ugly growth on one of its branches.

"It's got an ugly growth on one of its branches?" I tried.

"Exactly," said Yuri. "Hence the *terminalia* part of its name."

He went on to tell us about the bush in more detail. Apparently, it is a rather dim-witted example of African flora that has difficulty in telling the difference between the egg laid in its bark by an insect and its own offspring. Thinking the egg to be a bud, the proud but deluded parent plant pours all its energy into the "bud's" growth. Sadly, what actually happens is that this food nurtures a growth that forms around the developing parasite. The plant, mistaking the increasingly ugly growth for a flower, tries even harder and concentrates even more goodies into that area, meanwhile denying itself vital nutrients and growing weaker, sometimes to the point of death.

I think this parable is much less obscure than some of those that Jesus used. Occasionally, I find myself utterly drained by the insatiable needs of some people and events. They seem to take an inordinate amount of my time and energy. Sometimes I am quite sure that this is exactly as it should be. I don't know where we would be today if at certain times in our lives we hadn't been given permission to drain the resources of our friends, or they ours, and I am equally sure that God expects us to go many very exhausting miles for him. I'm sure you have experienced feeding and being fed in this way.

However, I do think there is a dangerous possibility that Christians, trying so hard to get it right, will become deluded like the silver-leafed terminalia. It has taken me many years to accept that occasionally we meet someone who is a parasite, greedily feeding off our energy until we are so weakened that we are no longer of use. At that point, people like this will often move on, looking for another confused, would-be "parent" who will mistake their apparently innocent and desperate needs for something potentially beautiful and therefore worth pouring out their lives for. I find this very hard to write, because I am so worried that people who have known me will interpret this as a comment on our relationship. But I can assure them that if they think that I am talking about them, they definitely aren't parasites, because parasites never question or doubt their motivation. They just feed.

PRAYER

Father,
You know how muddled we get when we are trying to do your will.
Please protect us from those who will use us up and spit us out,
and give us discernment to know when you want us to lay down
our daily lives and when you don't.   Amen.

2

Where the Heart Lies

The miracle of Lazarus being restored to life is so carefully stage-managed by Jesus and so inextricably bound up with his eventual arrest that it has always fascinated me, partly because, as with the wine at Cana, he has saved the best till last.

To raise a man from death a week after he has died is perhaps the most spectacular of all of Jesus' miracles. His relationship with the family, the proximity of Bethany to Jerusalem—allowing for the inevitability of the miracle's coming to the ears of the Sanhedrin—and the timing of the miracle to occur just before Passover all add to the unique flavor of this public demonstration of God's sovereignty.

Come On In!

As Jesus and his disciples were on their way, he came to a village where a woman named Martha opened her home to him.
LUKE 10:38 (NIV)

⟋⟍

$\mathcal{I}$ love the glimpses we are given of this little family. I'd give a lot to have been a fly on the wall while Mary and Martha were growing up. "As different as chalk from cheese," I can hear their mother say as she calms one stormy little girl and perhaps wishes the other could soften up a bit. Or praises the one for her diligence and despairs of the other's wild ways.

Now it's Martha's home, and Mary must have tried her patience something rotten. We don't meet Lazarus at this stage, but he's in the picture somewhere, and having had two sons who for a while couldn't be in the same room without rubbing each other the wrong way, I sympathize with his inevitable role as peacemaker between his two sisters.

We know something else about this ordinary family. We know that Jesus loved to pop in and eat with them when he was in Bethany. Perhaps it allowed him to feel off duty for a while, safely aware that what he said in their cozy kitchen would not be taken down and used as evidence against him. We know that despite his being seen by the crowds as a rabbi and a miracle worker and by the Pharisees as a major threat, Martha could speak to him as a friend and potential ally in her grumbling at Mary.

I wonder if they ever realized what their hospitality meant to this lonely Son of God while he was there or what a privilege it was to have Jesus as a close family friend.

Some years ago, I was involved in facilitating a self-support group for women who were experiencing particularly acute problems in their home lives. I was constantly amazed at the courage and resilience they showed as they battled day by day with circumstances that would have finished me off.

As the weeks went by, I was thrilled to see how well they were beginning to relate within the group and how openly they were sharing and advising each other. But one thing puzzled me. Despite their enthusiasm in supporting each other during the week as well as during our hour together, I discovered that they were not visiting each other in their homes. Distance was not the problem, as they all lived in the same neighborhood. Neither was time, as none of them were working.

At last I decided to tackle the subject. Apparently, they had all without exception longed to do just that, but felt embarrassed that their homes were not as nice as they would have liked them to be. One girl actually said that she had seen another member of the group crying as she pushed her two toddlers down the street and had longed to ask her in. But since she was out of coffee and milk she had just watched the woman through the net curtains instead. After all this mutual confessing, you can imagine that there was a good deal of relieved laughter. Some really useful friendships began that day that are still going strong today.

Fear of being judged and feelings of inadequacy affect us all, don't they? Perhaps if we could feel confident enough to invite those who seem far above us into the very middle of our family ups and downs, and if we could stop worrying about whether our home life is good enough, then we could give the same sense of belonging to another lonely child of God—Jesus.

<u>PRAYER</u>

Dear Father,
We so often feel that we are not good enough to have much of a
role in your plans. Forgive us for the times when we have let feel-
ings like this hamper your loving work. Help us to stop peeping at
the world through our net curtains and to throw open the doors of
our lives and welcome you in. AMEN.

Gracious Living

She had a sister called Mary, who sat at the Lord's feet listening to what he said. But Martha was distracted by all the preparations that had to be made. She came to him and asked, "Lord, don't you care that my sister has left me to do the work by myself? Tell her to help me!"

"Martha, Martha," the Lord answered, "you are worried and upset about many things, but only one thing is needed. Mary has chosen what is better, and it will not be taken away from her." LUKE 10:39–42 (NIV)

⁓ↄ

I remember one particular day in my life that I think epitomizes the ludicrous pressure that women sometimes find themselves under.

It was a Saturday morning, and I was in the kitchen. On the work surfaces were rows of iceberg-lettuce leaves, each containing two quarters of tomato and three slices of cucumber. On our wooden kitchen table was a large dollop of marmalade, a half-full mug of tea, and a plate containing the remains of a piece of toast. At the end of the table sat a disconsolate American eating lasagna, and next to me stood a small girl wearing my black petticoat and a hopeful expression while holding a long scarf and several plastic necklaces.

Before you even try to unravel the clues left at the scene of the crime, let me explain. The minisalads were the result of a rash promise I had made at a recent church planning meeting.

It was our church's fifth anniversary and we were celebrating it with a barbecue and fun day. I had suggested that instead of making one big salad we could prepare individual salads before-hand to make sure there would be enough for everyone. Of course, you should never suggest anything at a planning meeting unless you are prepared to do it yourself!

The blob of marmalade was a protest gone wrong. I had told one of my teenage sons that enough was enough, that I wasn't his paid servant and from now on he would clear up his own breakfast mess. That was fine as far as it went, but after agreeing quite graciously to do it in a minute, he had completely forgot-ten and had left! I felt I should still make a stand, so there the blob of marmalade had to stay.

The disconsolate American was a friend who had come to stay with us in order to work with my husband. The idyllic pic-ture he had probably savored of the two of them being serenely creative together was being shattered minute by minute, and on top of that I had suddenly realized that I'd forgotten to give him any lunch. He had to make do with the contents of the only con-tainer left in the freezer.

Lastly, the small girl was my daughter. That afternoon there was to be a fancy-dress parade based on characters from the Bible. For some obscure reason she had hit on the Queen of Sheba and felt strongly that my shiny black petticoat was exactly what the Queen of Sheba would have worn. By the time I had swirled the scarf round her head like a turban and she had cov-ered herself with "precious jewels" she looked somewhat vamp-ish, but by then I was too tired to care.

Why do we do it? Why don't we spend our time walking down dappled lanes or sipping Earl Grey on the terrace? Well, maybe you do, and if so, you'll have to give me the secret.

All I know is that life for many of us goes on at a ridiculous pace and we have far too little time to just "be." This wouldn't matter except that without our really noticing, the quality of our lives begins to deteriorate and we lose confidence in our ability to do anything. What's more, having worked ourselves silly to live up to some unseen expectation, we end up letting someone or everyone down by being so exhausted that we forget something vital. Or we feel used and become embittered, surly, and ungenerous with our time, forgiveness, and understanding.

Either way there is little left of the inner joy that Jesus promised us.

Throughout his time with us, Jesus recognized the need to remove himself for short periods of time just to be with God. Admittedly, all too often that time was interrupted, but he returned to work refreshed by this interval with his Father. Unfortunately, the self-imposed rule of a regular "quiet time" has become a pressure in itself for many people who feel inadequate if they fail to meet this expectation of themselves.

Time set aside to enjoy God in whatever setting relaxes us would be a nice thing to build in to every day. It could even mean a bit of dappled-lane walking. In the meantime, if ever I write my autobiography, it will have to be called *Fifty Salads and the Queen of Sheba*!

PRAYER

Father, please help us simply to stop.

Help us to learn how to relax with you, how to share our time with you. For those of us who have lost our joy, we pray for refreshment.

For those of us who have become hardened, we pray for a softening of our hearts and an increased understanding of your love for us whether we do things for you or not. Help us to choose wisely between the things that are important and the things that are of minisalad importance so that we can take control of our time. Draw us close to you. Thank you, Father. AMEN.

"The One You Love Is Sick"

Now a man named Lazarus was sick. He was from Bethany,
the village of Mary and her sister Martha. This Mary, whose
brother Lazarus now lay sick, was the same one who poured
perfume on the Lord and wiped his feet with her hair. So the
sisters sent word to Jesus, "Lord, the one you love is sick."

JOHN 11:1–3 (NIV)

∞

I have been to many different types of prayer meetings in my
Christian life and have prayed in many different ways for healing. One of my worst memories is this: a cold hall with a small,
uninviting circle of hard chairs in the middle and a tiny group of
the most pessimistic people you could ever meet. The list of the
sick and dying took a long time to read because it was punctuated
throughout by snippets of so-called news, which in reality was
gossip gleaned from bedsides with promises of secrecy.

That was bad enough. But it was followed by prayers spoken
in a depressed whisper that cringingly asked God for a scrap of
temporary comfort for the sick person as though the God they
knew was too busy or mean to be bothered with anything else.

One of my pet peeves is the type of praying that consists of
bellowing at God as though he were stone deaf, and demanding,
like petulant toddlers wanting sweets at the grocery-store check-
out counter, that the Holy Spirit come NOW. I'd never let my
own children get what they wanted if they spoke to me like that,
so I don't really see why God should. It seems so rude. I've ended
up in both those situations with a stiff bottom and a cross soul.

Not that it matters what I think. I learned that a long time ago from a friend who had visited America on business. He told us of an experience he had had in an enormous church in California. He said he had been sitting there amazed and amused by the pretentiousness of the event, at the artificial palm trees and massive bouffant pink satin curtains and the enormous choir dressed to kill. He said he felt very righteous. "What nonsense! How appalling! What must God think!" he thought.

Suddenly he found out. Amid the noise of singing and shouted prayers he heard the sound of crying, and turning around, he saw a young girl leave her wheelchair and dance for joy. Her parents were sobbing with incredulous joy. He saw other miracles taking place. There was genuine rejoicing and he realized that all the razzmatazz didn't matter to God so long as hearts were truly turned to him.

This story has stayed with me ever since and has helped me realize that there is no value in judging the way different groups worship. The key isn't in whether we have statues, crosses, cathedrals, or church halls. Nor is it the virtue of the guitar versus the organ. What God will see is the love in our hearts, and that will be beautiful to him.

So I don't think it matters how we pray. But from now on, I think I will pray for healing in the words Mary and Martha sent to Jesus. What better prayer could there be than "Lord, the one you love is sick"? Their decision to send for Jesus was mutual and immediate. No begging, no extraneous details, just a confidence that, as a close friend, he would want to be involved and that, because he loved them, he would do something.

PRAYER

Dear Father,
You know us so well. You know how in a crisis we sometimes erect
screens of panic that keep us from seeing you and we start talking
to you in these strange ways. Help us to remember what Mary and
Martha did. Increase our trust so that we can simply call you
when we need you, knowing that, whatever you decide to do, you
will have heard us.   AMEN.

Painful Silence

When he heard this, Jesus said, "This sickness will not end in death. No, it is for God's glory so that God's Son may be glorified through it." Jesus loved Martha and her sister and Lazarus. Yet when he heard that Lazarus was sick, he stayed where he was two more days. JOHN 11:4–6 (NIV)

⁓ᴏ

What must it have been like for Mary and Martha during the hours and then the days that followed the sending of their message? At first they might have wondered whether the messenger had arrived and talked confidently about what Jesus would do when he came. I can imagine them running to the window every time they heard footsteps, straining their eyes down the dusty road trying to catch a glimpse of their beloved Jesus. Then night would come and they would be lying in the dark, their ears straining for the sound they longed to hear. Then, gradually, their hope would give way to increasing despair as they watched Lazarus grow weaker with all the terrible symptoms of a fatal illness.

What did they think then? Did they question the whole basis of their relationship with Jesus? Perhaps he didn't really love them as much as they'd thought. Perhaps he thought their request impertinent. Perhaps they shouldn't have sent for him.

Many of us know all too well how they must have felt because we've been there. We have waited, we have hammered at the doors of heaven, we have despaired, and we have questioned whether the whole thing is some ghastly joke. Why isn't he here? Why doesn't he change things? Our confidence crumbles and all we can offer to the world is the salt of our tears.

Nothing in the world is more demoralizing than a long silence. Nothing seems to speak so eloquently of a broken relationship. Yet we know from experience how misleading our feelings can be. I don't know how many stories I've read to children about bunnies or teddies who think that everyone has forgotten their birthday, only to find (after sad tears into oversized handkerchiefs) that a surprise birthday party complete with ice cream and a giant pink cake and a forest of beaming furry creatures awaits them. And I have known many lonely people who have misread busyness as avoidance and laziness or disorganization as a deliberate statement of indifference.

For some of us it isn't that simple. There is no equivalent of a table bulging with party food. The mystery of God's silence remains painfully unexplained this side of heaven. But something in this part of the story just might help.

In the case of Mary and Martha, it turns out that it had nothing to do with their relationship with Jesus. It had to do with the small part they would play in the huge complicated plan that would end in the Crucifixion and the reconciliation of all humanity to their Father in heaven. What a mind-blowing thought! At the very point when we feel most deserted by God, we may be acting out the starring role in our scene of the play, the final curtain of which will be the Second Coming.

But even knowing that, it can still hurt a lot, can't it?

PRAYER

Dear Father,
Many of your children, even as they read this, will be screaming
inside themselves, "Why, why did you let this happen, God?" Few
of us will ever understand why life has to be so confusingly hard
for some people or why sometimes you choose to be silent. Please
help us to see that it's not because you don't love us to pieces. Hold
us close today, Father, and give those of us who stand by helplessly
watching and wondering the words of comfort and hope you
would want us to hear from you. **A**MEN.

Let Us Also Go

Then he said to his disciples, "Let us go back to Judea."

"But Rabbi," they said, "a short while ago the Jews tried to stone you, and yet you are going back there?"

Jesus answered, "Are there not twelve hours of daylight? A man who walks by day will not stumble, for he sees by this world's light. It is when he walks by night that he stumbles, for he has no light."

After he had said this, he went on to tell them, "Our friend Lazarus has fallen asleep; but I am going there to wake him up."

His disciples replied, "Lord, if he sleeps, he will get better." Jesus had been speaking of his death, but his disciples thought he meant natural sleep.

So then he told them plainly, "Lazarus is dead, and for your sake I am glad I was not there, so that you may believe. But let us go to him."

Then Thomas (called Didymus) said to the rest of the disciples, "Let us also go, that we may die with him."

JOHN 11:7–16 (NIV)

⌒◡

I have a horrible feeling that if I had been there I might have been one of the ones trying to persuade Jesus to stay away from

Jerusalem. I can imagine their bewilderment at Jesus' apparent determination to travel to his potential doom just to wake Lazarus up from what they thought was a healing sleep. Or did they? Did they really misunderstand Jesus when he said that Lazarus had fallen asleep? It is so easy to convince ourselves that our motives are completely reasonable when we are frightened.

A child who comes down with a bellyache before a worrisome day at school believes in that bellyache totally. The proof of the false illness can only be revealed after the school bell has rung and the child is at home, safe and cozy. Since children are not versed in subterfuge, wild bed trampolining is the most popular sign of the famous vanishing tummy ache trick. The headache we wake with before facing a particularly difficult day at work is definitely going to turn into a migraine—while if we wake with a headache before a day we are looking forward to we are sure that an aspirin will take care of it. I don't think that's villainy. But this sort of self-delusion can have more serious consequences.

For instance, I have far too often convinced myself that I have no time to contact an acquaintance, when the truth is that I find phoning anyone really difficult. Fewer ministers seem to hear God calling them to the inner city than to the suburbs, just as many people seem to hear God calling them to demonstrate in a controversial neighborhood but not to work in it. And from personal experience I can tell you that many people who work with disturbed teenagers find the sort of language they hear so offensive that they feel quite sure that they cannot continue to work in such an environment. We are so very fallible, aren't we?

The disciples were facing far more than a bad day at school or a swearing teenager. Thank heavens for Thomas! Don't you love the fact that it was this particular disciple, famous only for his doubting, who faced his fears openly and offered Jesus the support he needed?

PRAYER

Dear Father,
Please let the Holy Spirit come and sit beside us throughout this day and help us to look honestly at our motivation in all the decisions we are making. Please don't let us prevent anyone from doing the job you have for him or her because of our own fears, selfishness, or jealousy.

Thank you for Thomas. Through what we know about him, help us to see how easily we judge, basing our opinions on just one small part of someone's past behavior. Today could get a bit uncomfortable, Lord. But please don't let us get away with not being honest with ourselves in these areas. AMEN.

Let People Be Real

On his arrival, Jesus found that Lazarus had already been in the tomb for four days. Bethany was less than two miles from Jerusalem, and many Jews had come to Martha and Mary to comfort them in the loss of their brother. When Martha heard that Jesus was coming, she went out to meet him, but Mary stayed at home. JOHN 11:17–20 (NIV)

*I*n the wonderful children's story *The Velveteen Rabbit,* the toys Skin Horse and Rabbit have an in-depth discussion about what it means to be real. In response to Rabbit's question about whether it hurts to become real, Skin Horse replies, "Sometimes," and goes on to explain,

> "It doesn't happen all at once. . . . It takes a long time. That's why it doesn't often happen to people who break easily or have sharp edges, or who have to be carefully kept. Generally by the time you are Real, most of your hair has been loved off and your eyes drop out and you get loose in the joints and very shabby. But these things don't matter at all because once you are Real you can't be ugly except to people who don't understand. . . ." Rabbit sighed. He longed to become Real. . . . He wished he could become it without these uncomfortable things happening to him.

I have several friends who are involved with Cruse, a counseling service offered to bereaved persons. The counselors emphasize that no two people grieve the same way and so the key is to be true to oneself. Mary and Martha were equally devastated by their brother's death, but here is Martha, full of blinding indignation, rushing down the road to give Jesus a piece of her mind, while Mary sobs at home, needing to be alone in her grief.

I mentioned this to a friend of mine whose husband died recently and she immediately identified with Mary. Only six months after her husband's death was she able to be with people without fearing that she might break down. I know someone else who, the day after her beloved husband died, joined a volunteer organization because she needed to be busy and to be with as many people as possible. Quite clearly, there is no right way to grieve, and Jesus' reaction to both of his dear friends shows that he loved them and empathized with them equally.

PRAYER

Dear Father,
It is so easy for us to think that we know what someone else should do or feel because of our own reaction to a situation. Help us to clear our thoughts of all our assumptions and to spend time today listening to you so that we won't be so busy thinking of ways in which someone should act or be that we miss the tiny way in which we can be of real use to you. AMEN.

Let It All Out

When Martha heard that Jesus was coming, she went out to meet him, but Mary stayed at home.

"Lord," Martha said to Jesus, "if you had been here, my brother would not have died. But I know that even now God will give you whatever you ask."

Jesus said to her, "Your brother will rise again."

Martha answered, "I know he will rise again in the resurrection at the last day."

Jesus said to her, "I am the resurrection and the life. He who believes in me will live, even though he dies; and whoever lives and believes in me will never die. Do you believe this?"

"Yes, Lord," she told him, "I believe that you are the Christ, the Son of God, who was to come into the world."

JOHN 11:20–27 (NIV)

⌒⟲

I love this woman! Never again let her be denigrated. I love thinking of her tearing off her apron, letting the door bang closed behind her, lifting her skirts to run down the road to meet Jesus, and having it out with him.

In one breath she rips into her friend for not getting there in time to save her brother, and in the next reveals amazing faith in her master. The fact that Lazarus has been dead for four days might have justifiably dimmed her confidence a bit, but she says,

"I know that even now God will give you whatever you ask." Then she shows her understanding of the Scriptures and her prophetic discernment that Jesus is Christ, the Son of God.

I can't help wishing that we were able, like Martha, to run down the road and actually meet Jesus face to face when crises overwhelm us. Whatever Martha might have felt before she met him obviously evaporated in the solidity of his presence. Suddenly everything was going to be all right, because he was there at last.

I know lots of people, myself included, who have planned a few things to say to God when they meet him. Even as I write this I'm battling through a great deal of anger and confusion over the premature death of a dear friend, while all over Britain people are trying to come to terms with the fact that a gunman has just mowed down a classroom of primary-school children in Scotland.

I don't think there's much point in trying to come up with a neat spiritual solution to such a devastating, pointless tragedy. But I do think we can hurl our bewilderment at God. Where were you? How could you let this happen? Don't you care? Can't you see that this is the sort of thing that turns potential followers away and causes your little ones to stumble?

My only comfort in times like these is the knowledge that whenever someone actually meets Jesus in the middle of their despair, something about him restores their hope—and somehow inspires complete trust that he was in it with them.

<u>PRAYER</u>

Dear Father,
We need to talk to you today. We need to tell you in no uncertain
terms how we feel about something that has happened in our lives
or in the lives of our friends. Thank you for listening so lovingly to
Martha's honest and pained outburst. Please listen to us today as
we allow our deep feelings of bewilderment to be voiced, possibly
after a long time of keeping them bottled up inside us. Help us to
allow ourselves to be held by you at last. **AMEN.**

Jesus Wept

And after she had said this, she went back and called her sister Mary aside. "The Teacher is here," she said, "and is asking for you." When Mary heard this, she got up quickly and went to him. . . .

When Mary reached the place where Jesus was and saw him, she fell at his feet and said, "Lord, if you had been here, my brother would not have died."

When Jesus saw her weeping, and the Jews who had come along with her also weeping, he was deeply moved in spirit and troubled. "Where have you laid him?" he asked.

"Come and see, Lord," they replied.

Jesus wept.   JOHN 11:28–29, 32–35 (NIV)

*W*hy? Why did he weep? Surely he knew that everything was going to be all right for his favorite family.

Did he feel guilty because he could have prevented their pain by coming earlier, but because he needed Lazarus's healing to be a major miracle, they had had to suffer? Or did he weep because he knew that what he was about to do was the beginning of his own long journey toward death? Or because he knew, as God's Son, that whatever he said they would not be able to understand? Or quite simply because he couldn't bear to see his dear friends in such agony? Whatever the reason, I'm so very glad he did.

Sometimes, especially since becoming a parent, I find myself in a situation in which I know that someone's grief will only be temporary. I've bandaged grazed knees and tried unsuccessfully to mend favorite toys. I've cuddled to sleep a toddler devastated by the loss of a one-eared soft rabbit. I've attended funerals of budgies and hamsters. I've been helplessly aware of the agony caused by the betrayal of a best friend who chooses to sit next to someone else on the bus. I've touched fingers in sympathy after an unsuccessful audition. I've observed the dull grief of a small, mud-plastered soccer player who has just scored a goal for the opposing team. And I've been there myself.

I've slowly learned that passing on the knowledge that their grief will be temporary, in the form of "Never mind. You'll get over it," is useless and can be damaging. Yes, the pain will lessen in time. It may even go away completely. But right now they are hurting, and they can't understand, and nothing will ever be the same again.

If you are in that situation now, needing arms around you and needing to know that someone who loves you is sitting in the dark with you, remember that Jesus wept. He knew he was going to heal Lazarus. But still he wept. He will never minimize your pain. Just as he asked for Mary, who had shut herself away from everyone in her grief, so he is asking for you. Let him weep with you.

∽

PRAYER

Dear Father,
You know us so well. You know the pain that is bleeding its way
through our heads and hearts. You know the panic and loneliness

that comes from feeling that no one can or wants to understand. Help us to emerge from our dark corner and turn to you. Help us to tell you all the little things that she or he said or didn't say. Help us to look at you so we can see your tears. **AMEN.**

"Take Away the Stone!"

Jesus, once more deeply moved, came to the tomb. It was a cave with a stone laid across the entrance. "Take away the stone," he said.

"But, Lord," said Martha, the sister of the dead man, "by this time there is a bad odor, for he has been there four days."

Then Jesus said, "Did I not tell you that if you believed, you would see the glory of God?"

So they took away the stone. Then Jesus looked up and said, "Father, I thank you that you have heard me. I knew that you always hear me, but I said this for the benefit of the people standing here, that they may believe that you sent me."

JOHN 11:38–42 (NIV)

$\sim\!\!\partial$

Some of us have problems that stink. I know that this is an extremely distasteful image, but it is true. I have met people whose problems, locked inside their own personal tombs by seemingly immovable boulders, have been festering inside them for years.

Some people are all too aware that the poison is beginning to seep through the cracks and threaten their security—even their sanity. Others refuse to admit that something is behind the boulder and desperately camouflage the entrance, terrified of how they'd react if what was in there were ever discovered. Some have been convinced by others that their problem is not really deep-seated and that it could easily be removed if it weren't for their own stubbornness.

If ever there was an illustration of the statement that no problem is too big for God, this has to be it. This seems to be a test case for Jesus and an amazing visual reminder for the disciples, but it is also a reminder for all those present that God is a God of power as well as of love. They will need to hang on to this reminder over the next few weeks as they wrestle with the powerlessness of their Lord in the hands of the Pharisees.

Even before he arrived at Bethany, Jesus had stated that what was about to happen would glorify God. And he seems to have deliberately stayed away to create a situation that was apparently totally insoluble.

The reaction of the disciples is quite understandable. We react in the same way today. It seems that we still have a social code that determines what is acceptable to God and what he can and can't do. This reflects our feelings of inadequacy and our inability to cope. Where two or three gather together in his name they do rather frequently find that (surprise, surprise) they all know that God agrees entirely with their decision to ditch, postpone, or reflect blame for the problem onto the bearer of the problem.

I base this on years of involvement with residential social work. Here is the pattern: a child arrives who has displayed such appalling behavior in his or her last placement that a meeting has been held in which it has been decided that, in the best interests of the child (and having nothing whatsoever to do with the fact that the child has exhausted the resources of the social workers and has made them feel stupid), she or he should be moved to another establishment.

Upon arrival at the new home, the child is assured that his or her stay will be long-term and that this is the ideal place for him or her. Three months later, another meeting is held. It is agreed, with a deep sense of serious consideration for the child's well-being, that the child should be moved to another establishment—not at all, of course, because the child has exhausted the resources of the social workers and has made them feel stupid.

This isn't meant to be funny. Being considered too difficult to cope with may allow the child to feel a short burst of power and it will certainly give him or her a reputation that the child feels obliged to uphold. However, it will also increase the child's terror that what lies within him or her is so awful that no one will be able to help.

The result for the child is twofold: a terrifying escalation of the behavior that caused the expulsion, and increasing isolation from those in authority who have lost the chance they once had to roll away the boulder and deal with the poison within.

I have a young friend who has been made to feel like some sort of freak because her problem (which is not in any way of her own making) has proved too big for the leaders of her church. "They said they couldn't cope with me," she sobbed one night. "Am I so awful, so dirty, that not even God wants to know?"

Of course we don't always know what to do. I sometimes think I never do! Some people's problems are so deep-seated that they need someone who is skilled in that particular area to work with them—and then when they start trying to do something it might only make things worse. But this is quite a different thing from suggesting that God either can't deal with it, doesn't want to get his hands dirty, or doesn't love the person enough to want to get involved.

PRAYER

Dear Father,
Here we are again, out of our depth! Give us the courage today to
begin to roll away the boulder that we have placed over the entrance
to our deep-seated, unresolved problems and to allow you to see
into the darkness within. Increase our trust in you that you will
not be shocked or disgusted by anything that you will find. Help
us to believe in your love and wisdom so that slowly, and with you
beside us, we can begin to seek appropriate help and eventually
allow our lives to be washed clean in your waters of healing.
AMEN.

Please Take Charge

When he had said this, Jesus called in a loud voice, "Lazarus, come out!" The dead man came out, his hands and feet wrapped with strips of linen, and a cloth around his face.

Jesus said to them, "Take off the grave clothes and let him go."
JOHN 11:43–44 (NIV)

∽☉

*I*t's not easy being an onlooker. It's not comfortable feeling helpless. But what can we do to avoid the feelings of inadequacy that lead us into the sort of temptation mentioned in the last reflection? I've always struggled with this. My husband says that when he first met me I was rushing around after my friends with a metaphorical mop and bucket trying to clean up problems I had no hope of solving.

Several years ago, a dear friend went through the horror of her husband leaving her for another woman. Having been brought up to believe that a Christian marriage was bound somehow to work out, she was completely devastated. Why had it happened? How could God have let it happen? Where had she gone wrong? Why had no one told her? What sort of person was she, was he?

I felt so very helpless. I so much wanted to sort it out for her, to take away the agony that she was carrying and restore the confidence that had been shattered. In order to cope with her daily life and care for her child, she pushed the pain farther and farther inside and placed a boulder over the entrance as I helplessly stood by and watched. For once, my desperation led me to face my limitations honestly.

"I want to say that I'll be there for you whenever you need me," I said, "but I know that I won't. I know I'll let you down. I know there'll be times in the middle of the night when you'll be totally alone and desperate and I won't even be aware of it. I want to take away your pain but I know I'll say the wrong thing, do the wrong thing. I'll forget to pray. But I do love you and I will do my best."

It was the best thing I could have said. Both of us felt freed from the pressure of coping better than we were capable of. And I learned one of the most valuable lessons of my life. Yes, lots of situations are too big for us to sort out. We can't take away the pain. We can't perform miracles. But we can do lots of things to help roll away the stone.

Some of these things are clear from this passage. We can ask God to help. We can listen, watch, and pray, so that when the time comes we can join in appropriately with what he wants us to do. We can encourage our friends to seek expert help and become involved with the frightening business of looking for the first time at the source of the smell. If and when healing does occur, we can help, slowly and gently, to take off the grave clothes, the grubby remnants of fear and panic that still cling to them. Then we can trust and support them and encourage their independence from us. And we can be a friend, however costly that turns out to be.

◌

PRAYER

Dear Father,
Today let me stand back and allow you to take control of all
aspects of the things that trouble me. Help me to accept my role in
it all, handing you whichever surgical instrument you might need.
Please don't let me blunder in and mess up what you are doing
and please prevent me from offering more than I can manage, of
either expertise or time. Yes, Father, take charge of all that I do
today. **AMEN.**

Use God's Gift

Six days before the Passover, Jesus went to Bethany, the home of Lazarus, the man he had raised from death. They prepared a dinner for him there, which Martha helped serve; Lazarus was one of those who were sitting at the table with Jesus. Then Mary took a whole pint of a very expensive perfume made of pure nard, poured it on Jesus' feet, and wiped them with her hair. The sweet smell of the perfume filled the whole house.
JOHN 12:1–3

⌒⟡

*W*hat a heady mixture of joy and pain there must have been that night in Bethany! The two sisters had prepared a banquet to thank their dear friend, and seated with him and the disciples was the brother he had so wonderfully restored to them. So much to celebrate.

Yet how hollow their rejoicing must have seemed, aware as they were of the swelling atmosphere of hatred toward Jesus. It must have seemed so awful that it was coming from some of the Jews who had witnessed the miracle of Lazarus being brought back to life. How bewildering that something so obviously motivated by love would have proved to be the final straw for those jealous of Jesus' increasing popularity. Rumor had it that even Lazarus's life was at stake.

What would become of them all? Would this be the last night they would spend eating, talking, and laughing together around the dinner table; the last time Martha would fuss around

and wait on them; the last time a special silence would fall over
the room as Jesus began one of those wonderful stories?

Suddenly Martha's contrived normality proves too much for
Mary, who abandons all sense of propriety, impulsively pouring
her most precious ointment over the feet of her Lord and wiping
his feet with her hair. Oh, Mary, what else matters but that he
knows you understand, and what better way to show him that
you understand than to sacrifice your reputation and your most
prized possession in one glorious moment of worship? How
he must have loved you at that moment—not for what you did,
but just for being so *you*. The room was filled with fragrance,
we are told.

I don't know about you, but I've been in situations where
I've had in my possession a jar of priceless balm. I have pos-
sessed intuitively within me, at a particular moment, the words,
the understanding, or the gesture that could fill the room with
the fragrance of healing or compassion or forgiveness. But I
have chosen to bring my jar home unbroken. Maybe I was afraid
to make a fool of myself or I was unsure of how my gesture
would be received. Maybe I didn't care quite enough or I was
angry or indifferent or sulky. Whatever the motivation, I missed
my chance to perform a vital task for God, a task divinely suited
to my personality.

I don't think the church sufficiently celebrates the gifts of
the more impulsive personalities in its midst. These more impulsive personalities can be made to feel clumsy and inappropriate
in many situations where the Marthas of this world fit easily.
And their sins do often tend to be rather obvious. They don't
so much fall as plummet! But God has given them some of his
loveliest presents, knowing they will share them generously.
Being a bit of a Mary myself, crashing through life making
untold mistakes, I take great joy in realizing that on this
poignant night she got it absolutely right.

PRAYER

Dear Father,

Help us to look today at the contents of our balm jar. What do we have in our possession that we could spill generously for you? Have we deliberately withheld even one precious ounce of word or gesture that should have been giving comfort and support? We are so very sorry, Father. Please give us another chance to use the unique gift that you have given each one of us in the way you would like.

AMEN.

The Moment Is All

But one of his disciples, Judas Iscariot, who was later to betray him, objected, "Why wasn't this perfume sold and the money given to the poor? It was worth a year's wages." He did not say this because he cared about the poor but because he was a thief; as keeper of the money bag, he used to help himself to what was put into it.

"Leave her alone," Jesus replied. "It was intended that she should save this perfume for the day of my burial. You will always have the poor among you, but you will not always have me."

Meanwhile a large crowd of Jews found out that Jesus was there and came, not only because of him but also to see Lazarus, whom he had raised from the dead. So the chief priests made plans to kill Lazarus as well, for on account of him many of the Jews were going over to Jesus and putting their faith in him. JOHN 12:4–11 (NIV)

⁓ↄ

This is interesting, isn't it? Taken out of context it could give the health-and-wealth fanatics a bit of a boost—Jesus himself saying, "You will always have the poor among you." Pretty extraordinary. Surely Judas had a point. And yet, this is the same Jesus who throughout his three years of ministry sought out the weak, the poor, the suffering, the outcasts of society. The Beatitudes make it quite clear what he thought about the poor and vulnerable.

What we are seeing here is the glorious truth that every situation we find ourselves in is unique, however many times we find ourselves in it. And just occasionally we are going to be asked to step out of our normal routine and do something quite wonderfully bizarre, just as Paul felt it was right to change course completely and go to Macedonia when it made logical sense to carry on to Bithynia. So nine times out of ten it is right to obey the general rules of charity and common sense that are laid down over and over again by Jesus. This one occasion was different.

In 1995 we visited Soweto, a huge township on the edge of Johannesburg in South Africa, where we attended one of several daily worship meetings led by Nick Misupi, a Zulu Baptist minister who would later become head of the Evangelical Alliance in South Africa. Words cannot describe the surging joy, the heartfelt emotion, and the glorious, pounding singing that shook the mission tent, which literally bulged at the seams. When Adrian had the opportunity to tell the congregation what a privilege it was for us to worship with our brothers and sisters in Soweto, the roar of "Amen" practically flattened the tent!

Afterward, having received confirmation that it was all right to do so, we used up yards of film taking pictures of the church children. When we see their beaming, open faces smiling at us from the framed photograph on our living-room mantelpiece, we are reminded of that enchanting time.

One photo means more to me than any of the others. It is a photo of mattresses, chairs, radios, bikes, and innumerable other objects stacked to the ceiling in a little storeroom behind the tent. When Nick showed us this pile, his huge Zulu face shone with joy. Apparently, after each meeting the new converts (up to fifty a day) receive counseling. They are taught that the cost of following Jesus is huge and that as a symbol of their new life they must return all the goods they have stolen and hand in their guns.

The guns are handed over to the police. The goods are collected in this little room, and once a week they are burned as a symbol of turning away from sin and beginning a new life. Our whole family was profoundly moved by this, and Adrian wrote about it in the letter he writes regularly for the Bible Society. He received one very angry reply from a woman who felt quite upset about his condoning what seemed to her a waste of valuable resources. It was obvious to her that the goods should be distributed to the poor and needy.

When I read the letter, I was momentarily filled with confusion. What was Nick thinking? Immediately after I finished the letter I knew. The whole of his ministry and that of his associate pastors was committed, Jesus-like, to relieving the hurts of the poor. But to distribute these goods would have been quite wrong. They were stolen. They represented an old way of life. Turned in and burned, they stood for sin renounced. However useful a resource they might have been, on this one occasion it was right to waste them.

So, back to Mary and her precious nard. On this unique occasion, rules needed to be broken and the forthcoming sacrifice acknowledged extravagantly. Just for a moment, the poor had to wait. The moment was all.

And so it should be for us. For perpetually generous nard slingers there will be times when the godly exception to our rule will be to show restraint. For frugal stewards there will be occasions when pouring out the perfume is the right thing to do. Each of us will have God-given opportunities to enhance the occasions we find ourselves in, and the Holy Spirit will help us to discover what they are. But I think we may be surprised by what he will ask us to do.

PRAYER

Open our ears, Lord.

Help us to listen today to what the Holy Spirit is asking us to do for you, however surprising we may feel it to be.   AMEN.

Courage to Be Weak

Yet at the same time many even among the leaders believed in him. But because of the Pharisees they would not confess their faith for fear they would be put out of the synagogue; for they loved praise from men more than praise from God.

JOHN 12:42–43 (NIV)

Oh dear, I feel this really hits at the heart of the reason why most of us don't confess our faith more publicly. We all have synagogues that for one reason or another we don't want to be cast out of, and some of us even have our own personal Pharisee who would take great pleasure in instigating our removal. Obviously, for Jewish leaders at the time of Jesus, being put out of the synagogue would have had serious consequences. At the very least, it would have hardly been viewed as a good career move! For most of us, the worst that happens is that from then on we might be identified with the ridiculous stereotypes that television sitcoms excel at. So why does it matter to us so much?

A little while ago, I had an interesting opportunity to discover just how pathetic I am. I was taking a course to retrain myself as an elementary school teacher. It was the first time in some years that I had found myself among a large group of people who were not necessarily connected with Christianity, and I loved every minute of it. The only anxiety I had was that it was obvious from what several of the students had said that their overall opinion of the church was very low.

I felt a bit guilty, but I was so enjoying making new friends and being back in what felt like mainstream living that I convinced myself that just for once I didn't need to defend the church, so long as no one attacked what I actually believed. For some time, I had been thought of as simply an appendage to my husband's Christian writing and speaking, and it was just so nice being accepted purely for myself.

One morning, the subject of our lecture was teaching religious education. I was fascinated to hear what would be expected of us as elementary school teachers, but I was totally unprepared for the lecturer's first remarks: "This is a controversial subject, and before I talk in detail about what the national curriculum syllabus consists of, I would like to hear your views on the subject. I am going to go around the room and give each of you a chance to air your views."

Here it was at last—my opportunity to tell everyone about my faith. So why did I feel sick? Why was my heart pounding against my ribs and why was my tongue so dry? I was hardly going to be thrown to the lions. These people were my friends. Anyway, I was proud of what I believed. What on earth was the matter with me? By the time it was my turn to speak I was so nervous I could only whisper. Of course I was relieved after I had managed to state how important my relationship with Jesus was, and afterward I noticed nothing terribly different about the way people treated me. But I knew that a gap had developed. In addition to apologizing for anything they thought might offend me, they had a sort of unspoken sympathy for me.

I had become in their eyes one of those strange, sad people who rely on the prop of religion or have been brainwashed into believing something that others in their wisdom knew to be nonsense. I have a friend who has been involved for many years in abuse survival work. She tells me that the group will tolerate anyone coming to speak to them except Christians, for these very reasons.

I appreciate that my experience was slight compared to the horrendous aggression many Christians have to face in the workplace and at home. But I remember clearly enough the ridicule I sometimes had to cope with years ago as a child-care worker. Being associated with weakness is always difficult, and there is no doubt that for the vast majority, the experience of Christianity today is either seen as stuffy and irrelevant or as ridiculous and ineffective. On top of that, Christians are also trying to voluntarily lay down the weapons of aggressive response, and our new response of absorbing attacks and trying to forgive seems puny in the world's fluorescent light.

But maybe it's more fundamental than that. We all desperately need to be liked and accepted, and the fact is that you can actually *hear* the praise of men, while you have to *trust* in the praise of God.

PRAYER

Dear Father,
Help us to remember that we have something to be really proud of,
something worth being put out of synagogues for. Give us courage
to laugh in the face of demeaning insults and patronizing sympa-
thy. Forgive us for the times when we have left your side in order to
be accepted by a group of those who don't know you.   AMEN.

3

Yes to Adventure

In some areas of the Protestant Church, there is a sort of taboo against mentioning Mary. This seems a bit like throwing the baby out with the bathwater. In their determination to show how unimpressed they are with her position as the "most prayed-to saint" in the Catholic Church, they seem unable to look at her at all. When she is mentioned in a sort of obligatory way before Christmas, it is often her quality of meekness that is emphasized. The fact that she is usually represented in elementary-school Nativity plays by the smallest and sweetest little girl available does nothing to dispel this myth.

Even in the Catholic Church, Mary is perhaps most often praised for her docility. I personally think that she is one of the toughest and most courageous disciples that her son and Savior ever had. So let's give her a chance to teach us what being a child of God and a disciple of Jesus is about.

Yes to Adventure

In the sixth month of Elizabeth's pregnancy God sent the angel Gabriel to a town in Galilee named Nazareth. He had a message for a young woman promised in marriage to a man named Joseph, who was a descendant of King David. Her name was Mary. The angel came to her and said, "Peace be with you! The Lord is with you and has greatly blessed you!"

Mary was deeply troubled by the angel's message, and she wondered what his words meant. The angel said to her, "Don't be afraid, Mary; God has been gracious to you. You will become pregnant and give birth to a son, and you will name him Jesus. He will be great and will be called the Son of the Most High God. The Lord God will make him a king, as his ancestor David was, and he will be the king of the descendants of Jacob forever; his kingdom will never end!"

Mary said to the angel, "I am a virgin. How, then, can this be?"

The angel answered, "The Holy Spirit will come on you, and God's power will rest upon you. For this reason the holy child will be called the Son of God. Remember your relative Elizabeth. It is said that she cannot have children, but she herself is now six months pregnant, even though she is very old. For there is nothing that God cannot do."

"I am the Lord's servant," said Mary; "may it happen to me as you have said." And the angel left her.   Luke 1:26–38

*T*his girl should never again be depicted as docile. She was clearly young and she was a virgin, but docility and virginity do not automatically go together. Neither do docility and youth (I don't think they ever did).

In agreeing to this extraordinary request, Mary showed courage as great as any displayed throughout the Bible. Gabriel doesn't tell her that he's going to speak to Joseph on her behalf. He doesn't promise anything, actually. She is being asked to risk her marriage, her reputation, possibly even her life! Yet her response is a resounding yes. No fleeces like Gideon. No excuses like Moses. Just yes.

To challenge us without letting us know what lies in store for us seems so often to be God's way. Abraham had to set out on his long journey without knowing where he was going. Noah had to build a boat despite the ridicule of his neighbors.

Some years ago Adrian and I had the joy of meeting a man named David Watson, a popular evangelist writer, several times before his death. When we first met, he had just been diagnosed as having cancer. He described his slow but determined progress toward accepting the possibility that he might die even as he wanted desperately to be healed. He wanted to be able to say yes to whatever God had in store for him, and by the time we met him again he had done so.

"The best is yet to come" is the phrase we'll never forget. He had moved to a point where he was looking forward to death but was prepared to stay if that was God's will. He had chosen to say, like Mary, "I am the Lord's servant; may it happen to me as you have said."

As a woman, I find it very reassuring that God chose to deal directly with Mary. Joseph is not asked for his opinion first. Her father does not even get a mention. In some sectors of the church today, and based on an understanding of the husband's role as "head of the woman," many married women have been led to feel that their relationship with their heavenly Father is in some way secondary to that of their husbands. This leads them to believe that God is not likely to speak to them first, if he speaks to them at all.

Thinking this way can be terribly dangerous. Unless our relationship is directly with God, everything can easily get out of sorts. We can rely too much on our husband's bringing us news from God. We can end up bitter and resentful, and above all we can lose sight of our Father's love for us and of how special we are in his eyes.

Mary herself was spoken to, and it is clear from her reply that she already had a mature love for her Lord and a desire to be obedient to him, whatever the cost. Obviously, one of the reasons she was selected was that she was to be married to a descendant of David, but there would have been hundreds of such women to choose from over the years. No, quite clearly Mary was chosen because of who she was, and it was also quite clear that she had the option to accept the job or not. The fact that Gabriel only departs after she has spoken shows that her reply was important. It was not going to happen to her unless she agreed.

A few years ago I was in charge of a small youth group that met in my house after church. As a discussion starter one evening, I had prepared a questionnaire in which the members had to assign points from one to ten to things they hoped to have in the future. Included in the list were money, a career, a family, and adventure. I was stunned to find that one girl had given adventure no points at all. Nothing for adventure?

Mary, at much the same age, gave it a ten.

PRAYER

Dear Father,
We so want to be able to say yes to whatever you have planned for us. Please help us to overcome those things that prevent us. For some of us, it is fear of the unknown; for some, it is lack of confidence that you could possibly have a job for us to do; for others, it is that we haven't yet learned how to listen to you. Help us today to move a little closer to the time when we too can give ten points to adventure. AMEN.

Help Us Rejoice

*Soon afterward Mary got ready and hurried off to a town in
the hill country of Judea. She went into Zechariah's house and
greeted Elizabeth. When Elizabeth heard Mary's greeting, the
baby moved within her. Elizabeth was filled with the Holy
Spirit and said in a loud voice, "You are the most blessed of all
women, and blessed is the child you will bear! Why should this
great thing happen to me, that my Lord's mother comes to visit
me? For as soon as I heard your greeting, the baby within me
jumped with gladness. How happy you are to believe that the
Lord's message to you will come true!"*

Mary said,

> *"My heart praises the Lord;*
>> *my soul is glad because of God my Savior,*
>> *for he has remembered me, his lowly servant!*
> *From now on all people will call me happy,*
>> *because of the great things the Mighty God has
>> done for me.*
> *His name is holy;*
>> *from one generation to another*
>> *he shows mercy to those who honor him.*
> *He has stretched out his mighty arm*
>> *and scattered the proud with all their plans.*
> *He has brought down mighty kings from their thrones,*
>> *and lifted up the lowly.*
> *He has filled the hungry with good things,*
>> *and sent the rich away with empty hands.*
> *He has kept the promise he made to our ancestors,*
>> *and has come to the help of his servant Israel.*

> *He has remembered to show mercy to Abraham*
> *and to all his descendants forever!"*

> *Mary stayed about three months with Elizabeth and then went*
> *back home.*   LUKE 1:39–56

$\backsim\!\!\!\!\!\sigma$

It cannot be insignificant that Gabriel mentioned Elizabeth's pregnancy to Mary, her young cousin. We hear that Mary hurried off immediately afterward to find Elizabeth and spend time with her. In times of crisis, we all need someone special who will understand what we are going through. Sometimes it is a member of our family, but more often it is someone who is in or has been in the same situation as we are. Most support groups operate on this basis.

Mary has been told that Elizabeth is in much the same boat as she is. A miracle baby is growing inside each of them, and it must have seemed to Mary a literal godsend to be able to spend time with someone so able to empathize with her.

What a meeting it must have been between these two ordinary women bursting with babies and the Holy Spirit! What confidence must have flooded into the young visitor at Elizabeth's words. Here was confirmation that she had been right to trust the angel's message, that she really was to be the mother of her Lord.

This is a very special part of the whole story for me. I love the idea of the unborn baby John thumping about excitedly in his mother's womb. What a Spirit-filled character he was, even then. I love to think of Elizabeth, made young again by the pregnancy that (in her own words) had taken away her disgrace, ministering to a girl who would possibly have to face an even greater disgrace upon her return home. But in this text we don't hear about the potential problems. Elizabeth and Mary just rejoice in joy and praise.

I love Mary's girlish excitement at what was happening to her. But more than that, I love the fact that God gave Elizabeth and Mary this precious time together. Both women will lose their sons at an early age. Both will be deprived of the joy of shedding tears at their sons' weddings. Neither will be a grandmother. The sacrifice they will both be called on to make will be huge. But for now, nestled in the hills of Judea, they can be happy and safe.

PRAYER

Dear Father,
We know that in order for your will to be accomplished here on
earth, you need willing servants. We thank you for Mary and
Elizabeth, who dedicated their lives and the lives of their children
to you so completely. Help us to do the same when you want us to.
Help us to rejoice in the task you have given us to do, whatever the
cost, and thank you for the friends you have provided for us in our
times of crisis. AMEN.

Not Junk Mail ... but Reality

*At that time Emperor Augustus ordered a census to be taken
throughout the Roman Empire. . . . Everyone, then, went to register himself, each to his own hometown.*

*Joseph went from the town of Nazareth in Galilee to the town
of Bethlehem in Judea, the birthplace of King David. Joseph
went there because he was a descendant of David. He went to
register with Mary, who was promised in marriage to him. She
was pregnant, and while they were in Bethlehem, the time
came for her to have her baby. She gave birth to her first son,
wrapped him in cloths and laid him in a manger—there was
no room for them to stay in the inn.*

*There were some shepherds in that part of the country who
were spending the night in the fields, taking care of their flocks.
An angel of the Lord appeared to them, and the glory of the
Lord shone over them. They were terribly afraid, but the angel
said to them ... "This very day in David's town your Savior
was born—Christ the Lord! And this is what will prove it to
you: you will find a baby wrapped in cloths and lying in a
manger." ...*

*When the angels went away from them back into heaven, the
shepherds said to one another, "Let's go to Bethlehem and see
this thing that has happened, which the Lord has told us."*

*So they hurried off and found Mary and Joseph and saw the
baby lying in the manger.*   LUKE 2:1, 3–12, 15–16

⌒⌒

It is the middle of summer, and we have just completed a six-week tour of Australia and New Zealand. As I'm writing this I'm sitting outside a motel in Beverly Hills, waiting to be picked up for our first performance in America. We have been invited to perform our "Laughter and Tears," an evening of sketches, stories, and poetry, at three churches before setting off on the final leg of our journey. Today we lunched on Santa Monica Boulevard and went shopping in Universal City. How's that for cool!

Actually, I'm extremely hot, shockingly tired, unbelievably nervous, and a bit defeated. I can't find a hairbrush, we've lost all the postcards we've been carrying around for a week, and I've got several bulging bags of dirty clothes and no laundry facilities. Moreover, my internal clock is completely out of whack, as we traveled from New Zealand yesterday, leaving at eleven in the evening and arriving in the United States at three in the afternoon on the same day. Oh, and I'd do anything for a nice cup of English tea. Reality is very messy, isn't it?

I've now watched the American Christian Television channel for the first time. I've heard how weight loss, jobs, money, influence, and power can all be mine if I just say yes to Jesus. I've been given verses supporting this from just about every book in the Bible, and all that's keeping me from success is a teensy-weensy gift of money. So many words, so many promises. It reminds me of the junk mail that fills up our mailbox promising amazing offers on everything from double glazing to coffins. Or it's like those "personalized" computer-generated letters that inform us (in large print on the outside envelope) that we have won one hundred thousand dollars, which we discover (from extremely small print on the inside) means that we could be included in a drawing along with a million other "lucky" people.

Mary stands as a witness to the unreality of all this. As Adrian once wrote, God appears to have reacted in a somewhat bizarre way to the birth of Jesus, blowing the budget on angel effects to the point of not being able to afford a bed and breakfast for the chosen mother of his Son.

Her lifestyle was not enhanced one bit by her acceptance of the job God offered her. There were no special perks, no freebies, no bonuses, and no promises of long-term security included. This same lack of benefits came with the jobs of John the Baptist, the disciples, Paul, and even to those of us who today have said yes to being employed in God's firm.

Reality is very different from the fantasy world of Madison Avenue or Hollywood. It is very messy.

Here's a thought. If Jesus had been born in the inn, surrounded by cooing relatives, I doubt that the shepherds would have dared to go in and see him, especially when they were wearing their work clothes. But the Gospels are not fairy tales. The messy vulnerability of Jesus' birth set a pattern of extraordinary accessibility that distinguished the life of Jesus and is a mark of his closest followers.

PRAYER

Dear Father,
Thank you for reminding us that what you have always offered us is not what the world offers. Help us to distinguish between what we greedily want for ourselves and what we really need in order to bring ourselves closer to you. Help us to remain open to anything and anyone that you want to bring into our lives. Please use us in your service. AMEN.

Avoid Spillage!

*At that time there was a man named Simeon living in Jeru-
salem. He was a good, God-fearing man and was waiting
for Israel to be saved. The Holy Spirit was with him and had
assured him that he would not die before he had seen the
Lord's promised Messiah. Led by the Spirit, Simeon went into
the Temple. When the parents brought the child Jesus into the
Temple to do for him what the Law required, Simeon took the
child in his arms and gave thanks to God:*

> *"Now, Lord, you have kept your promise,*
> *and you may let your servant go in peace.*
> *With my own eyes I have seen your salvation,*
> *which you have prepared in the presence of all*
> *peoples:*
> *A light to reveal your will to the Gentiles*
> *and bring glory to your people Israel."*

*The child's father and mother were amazed at the things
Simeon said about him. . . .*

*Every year the parents of Jesus went to Jerusalem for the
Passover Festival. When Jesus was twelve years old, they went
to the festival as usual. When the festival was over, they started
back home, but the boy Jesus stayed in Jerusalem. . . . On the
third day they found him in the Temple, sitting with the Jewish
teachers, listening to them and asking questions. All who heard
him were amazed at his intelligent answers. His parents were
astonished when they saw him, and his mother said to him,
"Son, why have you done this to us? Your father and I have
been terribly worried trying to find you."*

He answered them, "Why did you have to look for me? Didn't you know that I had to be in my Father's house?" . . .

His mother treasured all these things in her heart.
LUKE 2:25–33, 41–43, 46–49, 51

⤳

*I*n the early years of our marriage, Adrian was completing his long-interrupted education, having returned to college to train to be a teacher. On one occasion he was way behind on a vital assignment, and I wanted to help.

"Let me help," I pleaded. "You dictate—I'll write." This conjures up such an idyllic little picture of wedded bliss, doesn't it? Forget it! For hours I sat, pen in hand, watching with increasing frustration as he stalked up and down our tiny living room, flicking channels on the TV, making and drinking coffee, and producing not a word. At just the point when I was ready to throw down the pen and go grumpily to bed, he said, "Right, here we go." He then dictated a two-thousand-word essay without stopping. He had written the whole thing in his head, including every comma and period. A process of slow percolation had taken place and the brew was now full of flavor, with not a drop spilled.

Many years later I was reminded of that evening. For a few months after he experienced his breakdown and until the stress involved in paying for it outweighed its usefulness, Adrian underwent analysis counseling. This period proved to be a great strain for me, because his counselor insisted that he not share any of his thoughts or feelings with me, but instead save them up for her. She called the process "avoiding spillage."

Difficult as it was for both of us, I could see her point even then. It would have been so easy for me to dilute the potency of his bad feelings by adding cupfuls of weak wisdom and "similar" memories. Teaspoons of comfort intended to sweeten the acrid flavor of the most bitter memories, although they might have made the time more palatable for us, could have disguised the poison and made it more difficult for the counselor to detect.

Now I see the same thing happening again in a different way. "That can't possibly work," "I just don't see it," or "They'll never buy it" are phrases that can greet a new idea Adrian shares with me and cause him to doubt its potential. Now he just avoids spillage!

Mary seems to have instinctively understood the value of avoiding spillage. Holding each new insight within her and allowing them to blend together and marinate slowly over a period of years must have created a rare maturity and depth of understanding concerning her son's mission. She knew she would need every drop of understanding to cope with the three years that would constitute his life's work here.

She was going to have to let him go and share him in a way few mothers have ever been called to share their child. There were going to be times when feeding on the memories of these early prophecies and incidents would be all she had to reassure her that he was in fact God.

When we are blessed with a tiny glimpse of the kingdom, whether through a word or a feeling, we might be wise to "treasure it in our hearts" for a while, to allow it to percolate through our system, seeing the experience as one herb in a bouquet garni, intended to subtly and slowly add flavor to our lives rather than provide a feast.

To share it immediately can subject it to a scrutiny that was not intended and to a superficial or slighting interpretation.

To hold it close and add it to everything else that happens during a particular period of time may help us form a clearer and deeper picture of what God is trying to communicate to us.

PRAYER

Dear Father,
We know there are times when it is right to share immediately the things we think you are saying to us. There are other times when it seems important to hold them close, to let them grow, to treat them as a part of the overall pattern that you are developing in our understanding. Help us to discern what we should do with the things you say to us so that we can avoid spillage where necessary and deepen our trust in you. AMEN.

Never the Same Again

*There was a wedding in the town of Cana in Galilee. Jesus'
mother was there, and Jesus and his disciples had also been
invited to the wedding. When the wine had given out, Jesus'
mother said to him, "They are out of wine."*

*"You must not tell me what to do," Jesus replied. "My time has
not yet come."*

*Jesus' mother then told the servants, "Do whatever he tells
you."* . . .

*Jesus said to the servants, "Fill these jars with water." They
filled them to the brim, and then he told them, "Now draw
some water out and take it to the man in charge of the feast."
They took him the water, which now had turned into wine, and
he tasted it. He . . . said to [the bridegroom], "Everyone else
serves the best wine first, and after the guests have drunk a lot,
he serves the ordinary wine. But you have kept the best wine
until now!"*   JOHN 2:1–5, 7–10

*Then Jesus went home. Again such a large crowd gathered that
Jesus and his disciples had no time to eat. When his family
heard about it, they set out to take charge of him, because people were saying, "He's gone mad!"*

*Then Jesus' mother and brothers arrived. They stood outside
the house and sent in a message, asking for him. A crowd was
sitting around Jesus, and they said to him, "Look, your mother
and your brothers and sisters are outside, and they want you."*

Jesus answered, "Who is my mother? Who are my brothers?"
   MARK 3:20–21, 31–33

*W*hat an amazing contrast there is between these two stories—they depict a radical change in both the nature of Jesus' ministry and in his mother's reaction.

At Cana we see Mary in control, sure of her ground, confident in her relationship with Jesus. I love the exchange: "My time has not yet come"—"Do whatever he tells you."

How proud she must have felt! How much she must have looked forward to the years to come and anticipated the fulfillment of the prophecies she had been hugging to herself for so many years.

Just a matter of months later, everything has changed. The sparkling trickle of living water sufficient to change water into wine has become a raging torrent, uprooting anything growing in its path, unseating established boulders of rules and traditions, rushing into uncharted areas of thought and relationship, swilling out dirt and darkness and ignorance. There is a wildness in this relentless flood, and for Mary it must have been shocking and frightening, apparently out of control.

Here, instead of being respected as a king, Jesus is accused of being mad and even evil. His brothers were clearly ashamed and anxious, going off to fetch their mother to get him under control. We don't know how she felt, struggling through the crowds, forced to send a message to her son via the jostling crowd, asking strangers to tell him to come out and have a word with her.

We can only imagine the shock, bewilderment, and possibly even humiliation she must have felt at his reply. Why did it have to be like that? Maybe it was the only way to break the pattern, to force her to face the truth and accept the separateness of his life as her adult son and as her Savior. What we do know is that her world—indeed, the world we have inherited—was never to be the same again.

We all have preconceived ideas of how God will do things. We plan our missions, our futures, our families around these ideas. We know what we would do if we were God, how we would go about things. Nothing prepares us for the times in our lives when the spiritual floods come. Familiar landmarks are in danger of being swept away and the landscape suddenly becomes alien and frightening.

At these times, we always have two choices with God. We can retreat to the banks, climb up onto dry ground, and remain safe but lonely. Or we can plunge into the raging waters of the Spirit and allow ourselves to be swept along in the biggest, scariest adventure we have ever had.

The living waters will unearth stubborn boulders of doubt, prejudice, and sin, will wash off the mud covering buried memories, and will cleanse and purify to an extent undreamed of. They will take us into areas we never expected to go at a speed we never meant to travel.

Mary had this choice. I have it. So do you.

And the only thing I am sure about is that if I choose that way, in the words of a Geoff Bullock song, "I will never be the same again."

PRAYER

Dear Father,
Help us to open our hearts to whatever you want of us, whatever
the cost, and to open our lives so that you can use us however you

want. Help us to choose your way, the way of the unexpected. Help us to let go of the banks and allow ourselves to be swirled along in the frothing living waters of the Holy Spirit, trusting in his direction and in his power. Amen.

No Fairy-Tale Ending

Then the apostles went back to Jerusalem from the Mount of Olives, which is about half a mile away from the city. They entered the city and went up to the room where they were staying: Peter, John, James and Andrew, Philip and Thomas, Bartholomew and Matthew, James son of Alphaeus, Simon the Patriot, and Judas son of James. They gathered frequently to pray as a group, together with the women and with Mary the mother of Jesus and with his brothers....

When the day of Pentecost came, all the believers were gathered together in one place. Suddenly there was a noise from the sky which sounded like a strong wind blowing, and it filled the whole house where they were sitting. Then they saw what looked like tongues of fire which spread out and touched each person there. They were all filled with the Holy Spirit and began to talk in other languages, as the Spirit enabled them to speak. ACTS 1:12–14; 2:1–4

$\mathcal{L}$eaping ahead past all the Easter events, here we find Mary again. This is a wonderful denouement to the story as far as she is concerned. She has seen it through from beginning to end, or perhaps I should say to a new beginning! Her son has become her Lord. She is now no longer primarily a mother, but first and foremost a disciple.

So what can we learn from her? Essentially, the value of hanging in there, of resilience, of loyalty. I can't help feeling that we, the church, have become a rather greedy bunch—at any rate, some of us have. Like fat little baby birds we want spiritual experience and we want it now! If we don't get it, we will, in the words of Violet Elizabeth Bott, "scream and scream until we're sick." We expect to receive a selection of the gifts of the Spirit in a starter pack as soon as we join ranks with the disciples.

We express our boredom if the church we are in is slow to deliver the goods. We moan if the sermon doesn't hold our attention or if the worship lags a bit. We change churches if the going gets tough. Please don't think I'm criticizing. I'm using myself as a reference point, as I've been there, done that. I've sought perfection and felt fed up when life has let me down.

Take last Easter, for example. We had been hoping to give the children who attend our Saturday club a little glimpse of why Easter is so special. I was helping a rather motley crew of children make gardens. If you didn't look at the huge pile of mud and chaos outside and only looked at the lines of foil containers, each containing grassy mounds, tiny wooden crosses made from split lollypop sticks, and an assortment of flowers, then you, like me, would have been enchanted.

The children were justifiably proud of their work, and I felt we had managed to create something of the wonder and perfection of Easter morning for them. We sat in a circle for our story about the Resurrection, and while I was telling it, I couldn't help feeling a little smug.

Suddenly I heard a yell, and when I looked up I saw two of my little gardeners engaged in something far removed from the peaceful atmosphere I had hoped to create. Locked in combat, snarling and yelping, they were slugging it out to the death over by the Easter garden table.

Abandoning Mary Magdalene to the mystery of "Who was that disguised gardener?" I rushed over and attempted to separate them. It was not easy, as it was clear that one of the most effective strategies they had learned in the school of life was holding on to large tufts of hair and pulling hard. Eventually, they stood before me gasping for breath, tears furrowing the layers of garden mud on their faces.

Jamie was first to explode indignantly, "Its not fair, Miss. He pinched my snail!"

"He did what?" As a reason for a duel it had to be one of the strangest.

"I had a snail, Miss, in my garden. He swiped it. Look, it's in his garden now."

I looked. Sure enough, Jamie's garden was snailless and a small snail reposed in the adjacent foil container. Irrefutable evidence. But even Watson might have noticed the fine line of silvery slime crossing the path between the foil rims.

"Was the snail dead, Jamie?"

"No, Miss."

"I think he may have walked onto Clive's garden, Jamie."

"Yeah, mine's better than yours, that's why," sneered a relieved Clive.

Before Jamie felt forced to justify the merits of his garden with his fists, I dragged both of them to the circle and somehow carried on with the story. The morning had lost its glow. But Mary would have understood. She knew about reality and she had lived her life doing what she thought was right at each stage of the way.

Some of it had been frightening, some of it wonderful, scary, amazing, humdrum, and appalling. She never quit, even when the going got horrible, and here she was at the beginning of yet another chapter. We don't know what happened to her after this. We don't hear of her again, but I would be very surprised if she didn't continue to lend her support and loyalty to the disciples. She's just that sort of person. One thing is for sure: her life hadn't been a fairy tale and this wasn't a neat ending. Life just isn't like that. The new churches would have their problems, the disciples would have their differences, and she would have her highs and lows. The church always has had them and always will have them, and Jesus never promised joy without pain.

But if people like Mary are around, there will always be the potential for new beginnings and continued growth, because there will always be someone around prepared to serve, prepared to say yes to life. And if that means wonderful gifts from the Holy Spirit, then that's all the better.

PRAYER

Dear Father,
Thank you so much for Mary. Help us to be more like her.
AMEN.

Some Famous Last Words

It seems that as Jesus approached his death, he felt able to talk more directly to his followers about the things close to his heart. The images are less obscure, the implications of his stories more carefully explained. We will only be able to look at a few of them, but I think that even this small selection reflects Jesus' positive message. By that, I don't mean the power of positive thinking. I mean the deep inner confidence of knowing that one is loved and valued through and through by a Father who is crackers about his children.

Lean Back and Relax

"I am the true vine, and my Father is the gardener. He cuts off every branch in me that bears no fruit, while every branch that does bear fruit he prunes so that it will be even more fruitful. You are already clean because of the word I have spoken to you. Remain in me, and I will remain in you. No branch can bear fruit by itself; it must remain in the vine. Neither can you bear fruit unless you remain in me.

"I am the vine; you are the branches. If a man remains in me and I in him, he will bear much fruit; apart from me you can do nothing. If anyone does not remain in me, he is like a branch that is thrown away and withers; such branches are picked up, thrown into the fire and burned. If you remain in me and my words remain in you, ask whatever you wish, and it will be given you. This is to my Father's glory, that you bear much fruit, showing yourselves to be my disciples.

"As the Father has loved me, so have I loved you. Now remain in my love."   JOHN 15:1–9 (NIV)

"**M**om, we've been having a lot of serious discussion, and we all feel that it's now or never for our band, so I don't think I'll be going back to the university next year." Silence falls. The air thickens with tension. My nineteen-year-old son and I look at each other. What do I say? What the heck do I say? Help! (Where's Adrian?) This is definitely a "lean back" situation.

I'll explain. Many years ago, during his early years in child-care work, Adrian learned one of the fundamental rules of dealing with an aggressive or threatening situation. Never leave the safety of your position or enter the fight on their ground. Always lean back, try to look relaxed, make yourself talk calmly, and pray! Now I'm not pretending that we've managed to do that too often during our own children's teenage years, but I do know that when we have managed, it has helped to defuse many a tense situation.

This was definitely such an occasion. Everything in me wanted to scream at him: "What about your future? Don't you care? How can you be so stupid? What about all the sacrifices we've made?" and so on. I leaned back, pressing my back against the cushions of the sofa. "That sounds interesting," I began.

Lean back. The image of the vine and branches means so much to me because it reminds me of this behavior. "I am the vine and you are the branches. . . . Remain in me. . . . Apart from me you can do nothing."

Whenever I get in a situation where I feel out of my depth (and being me that happens all the time), I try to remember these words. I imagine the Father standing behind me—strong, loving, and all wise—and I lean back on him in my mind, my arms entwined with his. I feel his strength, and sometimes even his wisdom and insight, ease into me, and I relax, secure in the knowledge that I am, in some way that I will never fully understand, plugged into his bloodline, the sap of the vine. I take such comfort in the fact that I am one of his branches, one that has often been buffeted so hard that it has nearly snapped, but nevertheless one that remains attached.

Have you ever wondered where the expression "sapping of strength" came from? I don't actually know myself, but I do know that when I rush into situations that are very difficult and try to cope with them on my own, I quickly use up my very limited resources. When I acknowledge my dependence on my spiritual Father and remember to lean back, allowing the sap of the Holy Spirit to flow through me, I am refreshed and strengthened, and I sometimes even bear a grape or two.

PRAYER

Dear Father,
When the going gets tough—for whatever reason—help us to lean back and revel in our closeness and familial attachment to you. Fill us with the sap of your loving-kindness so that our work for you doesn't dry up and wither. AMEN.

Walk in the Light

[Jesus said,] "Now is the time for judgment on this world; now the prince of this world will be driven out. But I, when I am lifted up from the earth, will draw all men to myself." He said this to show the kind of death he was going to die.

The crowd spoke up, "We have heard from the Law that the Christ will remain forever, so how can you say, 'The Son of Man must be lifted up'? Who is this 'Son of Man'?"

Then Jesus told them, "You are going to have the light just a little while longer. Walk while you have the light, before darkness overtakes you. The man who walks in the dark does not know where he is going. Put your trust in the light while you have it, so that you may become sons of light." When he had finished speaking, Jesus left and hid himself from them.

JOHN 12:31–36 (NIV)

❧

*E*very single night for months, I followed the same carefully thought-out plan. First, I would slide my cramped fingers free from their manacles, and then, without taking a breath, I would uncurl myself from my crouched position on the floor and rise cautiously to my feet.

From then on, as I moved slowly backwards, taking infinite care not to come in contact with the many obstacles I knew existed in the darkness behind me, everything depended on my intimate knowledge of my surroundings. The minutest sound, the tiniest squeak, and all would be lost. I had learned to slip silently out the door that I had surreptitiously left open a crack in preparation for my escape.

Then, heart thumping, I would wait for signs of stirring from the occupant of the room I had just left, knowing that recapture was all too possible. At last, breathing more easily, I would head for freedom.

Before you start to think that I am some unsung heroine involved in wildly heroic undercover work, I'll explain. The occupant of the room, whose waking could have proved so disastrous, was our two-year-old son Matthew, notorious among family members and baby-sitters alike for his inability to fall asleep without holding his mommy's or daddy's hand.

At the time, we felt ashamed of the ridiculous lifestyle this need inflicted on us. We were sure that we were the only couple in the world who took turns crouching patiently for hours in the dark, singing endless nursery rhymes and even simulating the heavy breathing of sleep until, yawning, miserable, and cramped, we might eventually be rewarded by the heavenly sounds of sleep-induced huffing and snuffling. (It was one of our most victorious moments when we met a couple in Birmingham who confessed that their small daughter couldn't sleep unless she had both parents lying beside her!)

We've since met many young parents who have suffered in this way, and the one thing we have all agreed on is that the key to successful escape lies in familiarity with the terrain gained during daylight hours! Of course, having an intimate knowledge of our immediate surroundings can help us in other ways too, not just in escaping from sleeping toddlers. For instance, it prepares those facing long-term blindness and provides them with a sense of independence and freedom. In this same way, Jesus is trying to prepare his friends for a time when they will have to make it on their own. In these final days, we see him pointing them forward again and again while encouraging them to gather all they can from the present. And as they look at him, what do they see?

They don't see long-dreamed-of trips to the equivalent of Florida, no settling of scores. Just the same consistent care for them they have always seen. The same constant, safe light that has steered them clear of so many rocks during the last three years. And he is asking them to do the same, to be children of light.

Recently Edna, a lovely member of our church, was hurled into darkness. Her husband, Colin, arrived home from work one day with a severe earache. By the next morning, he had been rushed to the hospital, unconscious, and he died a week later, never having fully regained consciousness.

As we gathered like stricken sheep in church on Sunday, the day after Colin died, our pastor gave us a message from our friend. The message was "I just want to tell you that I'm all right and Colin is very all right." Well of course she wasn't—and her grieving will be part of her forever. But we as a congregation were moved to the depths of our being that in the midst of her worst hour she had thought of those worrying about her. She said afterward, "I was so afraid that this might cause some to stumble."

Edna's reflection of the light had become a part of her and had quite naturally illumined the path of those stumbling after her.

PRAYER

Dear Father,
Help those of us who are not presently in darkness to appreciate
the full joy of being with you in the light. Help us to absorb the
light of your teaching so that however dark our surroundings
become, we will always have the comfort of your candle of hope
and love and the ability to illumine the path of your little ones.
A<small>MEN</small>.

Check Your Yeast!

"The kingdom of heaven is like yeast that a woman took and mixed into a large amount of flour until it worked all through the dough." MATTHEW 13:33 (NIV)

When they went across the lake, the disciples forgot to take bread. "Be careful," Jesus said to them. "Be on your guard against the yeast of the Pharisees and Sadducees."

They discussed this among themselves and said, "It is because we didn't bring any bread."

Aware of their discussion, Jesus asked, "You of little faith, why are you talking among yourselves about having no bread? Do you still not understand? Don't you remember the five loaves for the five thousand, and how many basketfuls you gathered? . . . How is it you don't understand that I was not talking to you about bread? But be on your guard against the yeast of the Pharisees and Sadducees." Then they understood that he was not telling them to guard against the yeast used in bread, but against the teaching of the Pharisees and Sadducees.

MATTHEW 16:5–9, 11–12 (NIV)

$\backsim\!\!\!\circ$

*I'*m about to show my age and discover yours. Do you remember ginger-beer plants? This question usually serves to separate the sheep among us from the lambs. Ginger-beer plants were a wonderful and almost mystical part of my summers when I was small. A mixture of ginger and yeast formed the base of the plant.

After it had doubled in size, you divided it in two and could give half away to someone else to begin their own cottage industry.

I can remember the pride I felt as I watched my mother place a lump of the smelly dark wet sand that was the ginger-beer plant into a jam jar to give to a neighbor. And I can remember thinking, "How can it be a plant at all when I know jolly well that plants have green leaves and grow in the earth in the garden?" How did it grow? How could something so horrid-looking produce such a lovely drink? Where did the bubbles come from, for goodness sake?

The ginger beer itself always seemed so special. I can see the glass-stoppered bottles now, standing on the cool stone flags of the pantry—and I can hear the awful explosion of a bottle that wasn't properly sealed.

Do you realize that I am talking pre-Coca-Cola days here? My children can't believe how we survived such tragic times. That my childhood was deprived of Coke does mean that I have a particular love for the very word *yeast,* and thus it is my favorite picture from the many that Jesus paints of the kingdom of heaven. (I don't have similar childhood experiences of mustard seeds, as I tend to associate them with saucers full of wet cotton wool growing the stuff you put in egg sandwiches. No birds would have ever been able to perch in those branches!)

Mingled with these memories are those connected with baking bread—lumps of stretchy dough to be bashed into shape on the kitchen table, then placed in the darkness of the pantry to secretly perform their magic. The bread pans with their glowing domes and heavenly smell. Tapping on the crust to hear the hollow sound that meant the loaves were baked to perfection. No wonder real-estate agents tell us to be sure to bake bread when prospective buyers come around! Yes, yeast has always received very good press.

That's why I find this advice from Jesus rather shocking. The idea of bad yeast is nasty. Bad yeast poisons the children of God, who acknowledge that they need bread in order to grow strong in their faith. The concept of bread that looks good but is in fact very bad for you frightens the child in me. But what a strong image to describe the danger of unwholesome teaching! Teaching like that of the "sinful Messiah," David Koresh, who led his followers to their tragic suicide. Teaching that condoned slavery and apartheid. Teaching that condemns those who do not receive healing as sinners. Teaching that looks good and may even taste good, but that is in fact the bread of death instead of the bread of life.

PRAYER

Dear Father,
We ask for your protection against the Pharisees of today. Help us to sift through all the teaching we receive and check the quality of the yeast involved so that no falsehoods will swell in us and we will smell sweet and be wholesome in your sight. AMEN.

Forget Your Toothbrush?

"Now I am going to him who sent me, yet none of you asks me, 'Where are you going?' Because I have said these things, you are filled with grief. But I tell you the truth: It is for your good that I am going away. Unless I go away, the Counselor will not come to you; but if I go, I will send him to you. When he comes, he will convict the world of guilt in regard to sin and righteousness and judgment: in regard to sin, because men do not believe in me; in regard to righteousness, because I am going to the Father, where you can see me no longer; and in regard to judgment, because the prince of this world now stands condemned.

"I have much more to say to you, more than you can now bear. But when he, the Spirit of truth, comes, he will guide you into all truth. . . .

"In a little while you will see me no more, and then after a little while you will see me."

Some of his disciples said to one another, "What does he mean by saying, 'In a little while you will see me no more, and then after a little while you will see me'?" . . .

Jesus saw that they wanted to ask him about this, so he said to them, "Are you asking one another what I meant? . . . I tell you the truth, you will weep and mourn while the world rejoices. You will grieve, but your grief will turn to joy."

JOHN 16:5–13, 16–17, 19–20 (NIV)

*H*ow can a tadpole know what it's like to be a frog—what it's like to hop and croak, sun itself on a rock and catch flies with its tongue? Presumably, if asked, the tadpole would opt for continued life as a tadpole and vigorously debate the advantages of pond dwelling. How could the disciples understand that something even more exciting than their nomadic life with Jesus was possible? Of course, it was frightening to contemplate.

In Australia recently, we were privileged to speak at a weekend conference held by an organization called Crossroads, which is committed to improving the quality of life of many physically and mentally disabled adults. Crossroads offers them adventure and inclusion in all aspects of life. The organization has taken group members all around the world, helping them face difficulties head-on, surmount the insurmountable, restore their dignity, and greatly improve their self-confidence.

The conference was a celebration of Crossroads' twentieth anniversary, and many of the delegates were extremely challenged, either physically or mentally. For some it was their first time away from the firm, loving structure of home and the rules that had helped them achieve a small level of independence. Being able to wash and dress and look after simple matters of hygiene had been hard for some of them to learn and had required continuous reinforcement over a long period of time.

Away from home, the delegates had to put their learned skills into practice, but a bewildering new routine made it difficult to rigidly stick to what they had learned. Hence the following conversation a friend of ours overheard during our after-breakfast speech.

"It's too long."

"What's too long?"

"This talk. It's too long."

"It's not. It's good."

"No, it's too long. Look, look at my teeth, they're going rotten, see? See? Look at them! They'll all fall out. They're falling out. See? See?"

The man was clutching his toothbrush, his face riddled with fear and panic as he frantically stabbed his finger at tooth after tooth. He was near tears.

How frightened he must have been. Clearly he had been taught that it was essential to clean his teeth immediately after every meal or else they would rot and fall out. Oh, he knew the score all right. He hadn't—and they would!

This transitional phase in his progress toward a life that would offer him undreamed-of adventure was confusing and a bit lonely and scary, but clearly essential. His respect for what he had learned so far would not disappear because he was learning that rules can sometimes be broken; instead, it was hoped that he would discover that, while good habits are essential, real security is found in relationships rather than rules.

What would be the next stop for him? The London Underground? Big Ben? The Eiffel Tower?

For the disciples? The releasing of the Holy Spirit, the discovery that Jesus dwelled so deeply in their hearts that he would never leave them, and a ministry of healing and teaching and church planting as yet undreamed of.

For us? It will vary for each one of us, but if we do want to be a part of the adventure God has specifically planned for us, it might be useful to think today of what it is we are clutching. Where does our security lie? What principles and traditions are binding us?

The teaching that man had received about brushing his teeth had not been wrong in itself. But it wasn't the whole truth, and at that stage in our delegate's life it needed to be reexamined and explained in more detail.

What needs to be reconsidered in our own lives in order for us to be able to move toward a life of greater spiritual independence?

Whatever it is, we, like Jesus' disciples, will need convincing that the truth as we know it is not the whole truth.

PRAYER

Dear Father,
Open our hearts and minds to the truth, the whole truth, and
nothing but the truth. Help us to become aware today of those
things that we need to look at afresh and learn more about in
order to move on in our life's adventure. Please don't let our fears
and self-made rules get in the way. Teach us the next step toward
independent Jesus-living so that we can learn to live securely in
you and allow you to live in us. AMEN.

Real Quality Control

"I have revealed you to those whom you gave me out of the world. They were yours; you gave them to me and they have obeyed your word. Now they know that everything you have given me comes from you. For I gave them the words you gave me and they accepted them. They knew with certainty that I came from you, and they believed that you sent me. I pray for them. I am not praying for the world, but for those you have given me, for they are yours. All I have is yours, and all you have is mine. And glory has come to me through them. I will remain in the world no longer, but they are still in the world, and I am coming to you. Holy Father, protect them by the power of your name—the name you gave me—so that they may be one as we are one. While I was with them, I protected them and kept them safe by that name you gave me."

John 17:6–12 (NIV)

$\backsim\!\!\partial$

$\mathcal{R}$ecently we had coffee with some friends who help run a community church in a nearby town. They were pretty devastated by a meeting they had had with the leaders of a huge charismatic church that had been established nearby. I listened to some of the opinions they were voicing and felt that the whole argument seemed familiar.

"The thing is," one of our friends said, "he compared our roles as being like the difference between the supermarket outside town and the corner shop. He said that they were planning to bus people in from nearby towns and that he saw their role as supplying a huge variety of whatever spiritual needs people needed. What does that say about us? I just don't see how we can compete. Who will still want to come to us when they can get really lively worship and famous visiting speakers just down the road?"

Of course! I'd heard these arguments before at a protest meeting held by shopkeepers in our small market town when one of the supermarket giants was proposing to build a branch on the outskirts of town.

"It will draw all the trade from the town center and more shops will die. . . . It will remove all the life, color, and atmosphere and make what we do have in the town seem dull. . . . We can't compete with their displays . . . variety . . . prices. . . . What about all the old, sick, and poor who don't have transportation and can't make it out there?"

The same arguments. The same perhaps well-grounded fears.

So what happens if we examine the arguments in the light of our friends' situation?

There are some wonderful big churches around, with exciting worship bands, imaginative children's work, dynamic youth groups, excellent preaching, and confident opportunities to receive the Holy Spirit. They are as much fun to visit as the huge, exciting supermarket. There are all sorts of good reasons for attending such a church, and fears and prejudices of small-church members are often unjustified.

But there are dangers. Sometimes the big churches are insensitive to the long-term effects of their presence on the local community. Sometimes life is drawn out of the local churches, and those who leave their local churches aren't often encouraged to remain involved at a local level. This can leave the local church feeling hurt and de-skilled.

Then there is "quality," as Jesus would have meant it. In both stores the quality and variety of goods is excellent and the packaging is very attractive. But at what cost? Where are the irregular-shaped apples and knobbly carrots? Anyone who has ever done a stint in a supermarket knows the answer: They are rejected automatically because they sully the store's overall perfect look.

The same thing happens in some churches, where those whose emotional shape has been deformed by encounters with stones while growing up are rejected and made to feel less worthy than those whose outward appearance is more acceptable. This represents a serious waste of resources and, as far as the church is concerned, can be appallingly cruel. I have bought many glossy apples that are soft and powdery inside, and home-grown knobbly carrots have the best flavor.

A huge supermarket, with its mindless and endless music, is impersonal. The supermarket is not where I run in an emergency. It's not where I bump into people I know. It's not where I know the manager and share in his or her life in any way. It's not "mine" and doesn't need my input. Can this be applied to the church situation?

Jesus brings "Those you have given me" to his Father and sets a pattern for church life that the disciples go on to emulate. It is a safe community where the vulnerable are cared for, the young can grow, and the needs of each member are of paramount importance to the leaders.

If the huge churches are doing these things, then they will be sensitive to the needs of little local churches and see that part of their job is offering them support. If the small local churches are doing these things, they will see that part of their job is praying for and befriending those working in the big churches. They will comfortably recognize what they can gain from coming in contact with lively worship and will feel free to encourage their young to get involved. What will not work is suspicion and anger on the one hand and greed and insensitivity on the other.

The only thing that really matters is that when we get to heaven we will be able to say, "I have revealed you to those whom you gave me." Have we?

PRAYER

Dear Father,
Please show me today those whom you have given me to love and care for. Please forgive me for the times I have forgotten to pray for them and help me to take more responsibility for their relationship with you.   AMEN.

Open the Packet

Jesus replied, "The hour has come for the Son of Man to be glorified. I tell you the truth, unless a kernel of wheat falls to the ground and dies, it remains only a single seed. But if it dies, it produces many seeds. The man who loves his life will lose it, while the man who hates his life in this world will keep it for eternal life. Whoever serves me must follow me; and where I am, my servant also will be. My Father will honor the one who serves me.

"Now my heart is troubled, and what shall I say? 'Father, save me from this hour'? No, it was for this very reason I came to this hour. Father, glorify your name!" JOHN 12:23–28 (NIV)

~~⌒~~

Springtime when I was a small child meant proudly assisting in the planting of beans. I was Holder-Opener of the packet and Bean Selector. My father was Hole Maker and Planter General. Together over the weeks that followed the planting of the beans, we were Progress Inspectors. I remember being tremendously impressed by the size of the plant that could grow from one tiny seed and the number of beans he and I could pick from the patch of garden where they were nurtured. The miracle of life that in turn produces life was as powerful an image then as now.

It is in this context of procreation that Jesus presents the idea of dying to self. I find this interesting. Somehow, I had always associated the idea of hating one's life with self-denial and even self-destruction. I found it confusing that my creator should want me to hate the life he had created. But here we see him suggesting that glory lies in the giving of self, that in this way blessings will multiply and a new and more vigorous life will flourish, whereas hugging life to oneself is inevitably sterile. But acknowledging the barrenness of our present situation doesn't always make handing over control of our lives easy. It seems it has to cost something to be worthy of the giving. We have to accept that the hour we have come to is the very one that was planned for us so that God might be glorified, and that can be hard.

There have been times in my life, as I'm sure there have been in yours, when I have found this very hard, times that feel as if they cannot possibly be part of what a loving Father would have intended for me as one of his children.

I have learned that the first thing I have to do at these times is look clearly at what is happening. I often have to accept the hard fact that the circumstances surrounding me aren't going to change and that it is up to me to stop bashing on the walls of my prison (an exhausting and futile business). I must begin to face up to the change in myself that is essential if I'm going to be able to adapt to new circumstances.

A friend of ours said recently that she had come to realize that most decisions are between what you don't want and what you *really* don't want. For example, although I was feeling very unhappy and confused when I was experiencing difficulties with Adrian's job, I really didn't want to ruin the work God had given Adrian to do. And I really didn't want our relationship to be spoiled and I really missed my sense of closeness with God and I hated feeling guilty.

At first I tried to change myself, to willfully superimpose acceptance onto my then state of mind while still holding fast to the closed packet of my life. This failed totally, and I became increasingly bitter and unhappy.

Eventually, I turned back to my Father in heaven, and in an atmosphere of familiar closeness with my Lord I was able at last to open the packet of pain I had been clutching to me. I even managed to take out a bean or two and give them to him to be planted. My packet is still half full, I'm afraid (although maybe heaven is rejoicing that it's half empty). Still, it's pretty exciting waiting to see what crop will grow from those beans I have been able to entrust to him.

Perhaps for you it will be a cataclysmic crisis that will allow you to give over control of your life. Maybe it has already happened. But if, like me, you are still finding this difficult, remember that the first step is to open the packet.

PRAYER

Dear Father,
Show us how to begin to give you our lives. Be close to us today so
that in your presence we can peep at some of the things that are
troubling us. Help us to take one bean out of our packet today.
Help us to stretch out our hand and give it to you. Help us to trust
that you have taken it. Give us courage not to take it back, not to
close the packet, so that at last our beans can be sown and in time
produce a useful crop. AMEN.

A Promise of Welcome

Simon Peter asked him, "Lord, where are you going?"

Jesus replied, "Where I am going, you cannot follow now, but you will follow later."...

"Do not let your hearts be troubled. Trust in God; trust also in me. In my Father's house are many rooms; if it were not so, I would have told you. I am going there to prepare a place for you. And if I go and prepare a place for you, I will come back and take you to be with me that you also may be where I am. You know the way to the place where I am going."

Thomas said to him, "Lord, we don't know where you are going, so how can we know the way?"

Jesus answered, "I am the way and the truth and the life. No one comes to the Father except through me. If you really knew me, you would know my Father as well. From now on, you do know him and have seen him." JOHN 13:36, 14:1–7 (NIV)

She felt so incredibly exhausted. So tired, so bruised with pain and confusion, so desperately alone. And it was so dark, the territory so unfamiliar. She clutched her sadness and fear to her—they were all she had.

She thought of her family. They had been so angry and had shed so many tears when they found out that she had to leave them. It had seemed so unfair to them. Explanations had proved useless. Only her husband had really wished her well and told her not to worry, that she'd see him soon.

Well, no turning back now or ever again. Never to see the familiar things that had meant so much, the furniture that she and her husband had lovingly collected over the years. Never to smell burnt toast, wallflowers, baby's talcum powder. Never to hold or touch those she'd loved so much. Never to hear the dog barking at the postman or the milk bottles jingling as they were placed on the step or the children's music blaring from behind their closed doors. Imagine, she was even missing that now.

So alone.

A stranger's voice calling her name, calm and real and somehow familiar. Where was it coming from? Who . . . ?

She began to run, strength flooding into muscles she had thought were wasted. The air smelled of spring and sea and baking and home. Dawn was coming, birds were waking.

And there he was, standing, waiting. Arms wide, waiting for her—for her. Now she was running, laughing, crying—flinging herself into the safety of his arms. Everything was going to be all right. She was home at last.

And Jesus, his arm around the most recently arrived member of his family, strolled with her into heaven to introduce her proudly to the Father she had never met but would recognize immediately.

That's the promise, a promise of a room prepared. A promise of welcome. A promise of a Father whom we will recognize because we have met his Son.

It's also the knowledge that Jesus has taken the same route. The same step into darkness. The same prayers to take away the necessity for the journey. The same aloneness. He has already marked the path, trodden down the brambles. He is the way. If we follow the path he has directed us onto he will meet us and accompany us into heaven.

What a promise!

PRAYER

Lord, this is the hardest journey.

Give those who are now traveling that way the reassurance of your presence beside them at every step. And help the rest of us, in our anger and our tears. AMEN.

"God So Loved the World..."

We have reached the point of following Jesus to his death. My prayer for all of us is that we hold the Father's hand as we remember all that Jesus went through for us. I suggest this partly because we need his support, but also because it is a very special chance for us to allow into our minds the concept of a vulnerable father, grieving for his son, yet helpless through his own love for us to intervene in the inevitable, horrific course of events.

The Choice Is Ours

"My command is this: Love each other as I have loved you. Greater love has no one than this, that he lay down his life for his friends. You are my friends if you do what I command. I no longer call you servants, because a servant does not know his master's business. Instead, I have called you friends, for everything that I learned from my Father I have made known to you." JOHN 15:12–15 (NIV)

$\qquad \qquad \qquad \qquad$ ❦

*W*e are coming into the long, dark shadow of the cross. From the moment Jesus enters Jerusalem, we know his destiny is set. He has chosen. He has said yes to the hardest request ever to be asked of anyone. He himself has chosen to demonstrate that the greatest thing we can do is lay down our lives for our friends.

We are not going to join those who arrived at the foot of the cross once it was standing on the hill. It is so easy for us to skip over the ghastly chapter in Jesus' life. Some churches even encourage us to do so, feeling that we should now concentrate on the happy ending. To skip to the last chapter of any book, especially one with a horrifying or tense plot, might be safe or cozy, but it will mean little to us.

We need to enter fully into the living hell of that terrible week. We need to ban from our minds for a while all images of the glorious risen Lord. This is not an actor playing a part who will, at the end of the workday, return to his flat for crumpets and hot chocolate. These are the last days in the life of a man.

Of course we know he was also God, but he has chosen to be as powerless and as despairing as any of us would have been.

Do we have the courage to walk with him? It doesn't seem much to ask of ourselves, considering what he has chosen to do for us. Let's go join the crowds at the gate of Jerusalem.

<hr/>

MEDITATION

We are walking toward Jerusalem. We are silent, afraid. There is something in the air, a new sense of determination in the silent figure we are following. He stops. He looks toward Jerusalem. He says something to those near enough to hear. He appears to be weeping. We have a choice. We can go with him or we can quite simply turn away and go home, home to where it's safe, where there are no triumphant glances and whispered confidences passing between the Pharisees, no stench of danger. We can leave. Or we can follow. We can be there for the dear familiar person who has brought us so much laughter and joy. Shall we follow? Shall we leave? The choice is ours. After all, we are no longer servants. We are his friends.

Wanted: One Donkey

The next day the great crowd that had come for the Feast heard that Jesus was on his way to Jerusalem. They took palm branches and went out to meet him, shouting,

"Hosanna!"

"Blessed is he who comes in the name of the Lord!"

"Blessed is the King of Israel!"

Jesus found a young donkey and sat upon it, as it is written,

> *"Do not be afraid, O Daughter of Zion;*
> *see, your king is coming,*
> *seated on a donkey's colt."*

At first his disciples did not understand all this. Only after Jesus was glorified did they realize that these things had been written about him and that they had done these things to him.

Now the crowd that was with him when he called Lazarus from the tomb and raised him from the dead continued to spread the word. Many people, because they had heard that he had given this miraculous sign, went out to meet him. So the Pharisees said to one another, "See, this is getting us nowhere. Look how the whole world has gone after him!"

JOHN 12:12–19 (NIV)

℘

*F*rom childhood we are taught that Jesus came to save us, that in order to reconcile us to the Father by taking on our sins he had to die. Yet it was in life as well as death that he sought to reconcile us, by communicating the truth about the Father in as many ways as he could. In his last few days of freedom, we see an urgency that is unparalleled in the rest of his ministry.

Here, on the day we now call Palm Sunday, we see him using an opportunity to the fullest extent. He knew that hundreds of people would be in Jerusalem because of the Passover and that news of his recent miracle had reached them. He knew that they would be there in droves to see the miracle maker for themselves (after all, he always understood our human nature perfectly). He had every intention of using this photo opportunity to the fullest extent. In front of this vast chanting crowd, words without a microphone would be useless. So he chose a visual aid. No high-tech phenomenon: just a little donkey's colt.

Have you ever, as an adult, sat on a rocking horse or crushed yourself into a kindergarten chair? It doesn't take a sociological analysis to know that it looks and feels pretty ridiculous. So why did he do it—apart from giving the learned a cryptic clue as to his identity and all who would live after him reassurance that Scripture had been fulfilled? The reason has to lie in the words from the relevant passage in Zechariah. "Do not be afraid, O Daughter of Zion; see, your king is coming, seated on a donkey's colt." Jesus is clearly determined to show himself—and through himself the Father—as vulnerable and accessible. So what has gone wrong? Why do we represent him in so many strange ways?

A few years ago I was profoundly affected by a poem I read by Steve Turner called "How to Hide Jesus." The gist of the poem was that we had successfully hidden Jesus from the masses, not by chaining up Bibles so that people couldn't read them, but by the strange dress, language, and behavior of his modern representatives.

Recently I met a woman who had been through an appalling experience. We had been told what had happened to her and felt very sympathetic.

"Has it been awful?" I asked.

"Well, no," she said with a bright smile. "It's been a growing time."

I later found out that she had allowed no one into her pain because she had been taught by evangelists to always pass on the good things that God was doing in her life. In her obedient attempt to give God a good reference, she had cut herself off from the help that she needed, and she was in danger of falling apart.

My fear is that our ridiculous need to represent Jesus by the successes in our own lives—materially and emotionally—actually hides him from those who need him. Suppose I have gotten myself into a real mess, and I'm not a Christian, and I live next door to a woman who seems to be successful in all those ways. How can I possibly tell her about the mess that I'm in? Surely she couldn't possibly understand: she's got her life so together. Surely the God she worships would have no time for a failure like me. Wouldn't I be more inclined to seek the help of a fellow sinner or a secular professional than to open myself to my Christian neighbor?

But if I knew that however much you have fouled up, God still loves you and has never let you go, then I might dare to think that maybe he would be the same with me. Perhaps we need to find ourselves the equivalent of a donkey's colt so that present-day daughters (and sons) of Zion need not be afraid of their king.

PRAYER

Dear Father,
Help me today to look for ways in which I can proclaim your love to those who up till now have only heard the rumors. Help me to be vulnerable in my dealings with those who don't know you yet—so that they can see you in me and not just the badly drawn picture of you that my life portrays. Help me to let those who don't know that you'll play a real role in my life from now on. AMEN.

Help Us to Question

"What shall I do, then, with the one you call the king of the Jews?" Pilate asked them.

"Crucify him!" they shouted.

"Why? What crime has he committed?" asked Pilate.

But they shouted all the louder, "Crucify him!"

Wanting to satisfy the crowd, Pilate released Barabbas to them. He had Jesus flogged, and handed him over to be crucified.

The soldiers led Jesus away into the palace (that is, the Praetorium) and called together the whole company of soldiers. MARK 15:12–16 (NIV)

⟅⟆

After the judge delivered the sentence—"You will go to the cross"—a sequence of events was prescribed. First, the condemned man was to be removed from view.

We often sing, "Just a Closer Walk with Thee." If you're anything like me, you probably picture yourself meandering down a country lane in the warm afternoon sun picking off heads of corn and listening to the master storyteller. But walking closely with Jesus into that closed courtyard and waiting for the company of soldiers would have been quite simply terrifying.

I wonder what the soldiers saw, if they bothered to look into their captive's face—the man so human that the nonreligious felt they could ask him to come for a beer down at the corner bar? The friend with whom women felt free to be themselves without the risk of being misunderstood? The adult so cozy that children rushed to hug him when they saw him? The man whose story-telling had been so spellbinding that the temple guards returned to the furious Pharisees without their prisoner? Their only defense was "Never did a man speak as he speaks."

I don't think they saw any of that, not just because Jesus had chosen powerlessness, but also because of the effect a death sentence can have on those closely involved. Looking at him, they would have seen a person whose identity had been removed, a person with no rights or choices, an object rather than a human being.

What is so frightening is that however much I may condemn the soldiers for their response, I know that I too have been guilty of accepting without question the sentences placed on other individuals. Character assassination in the newspapers can result in the death of a promising career, emotional torture, the destruction of relationships, and even suicide.

Perhaps there is nothing I can do about that, but what about the times when I allow all the good and true things I know about someone to slip to the very back of my mind so that I can enjoy a good gossip? Or the times when I accept an embittered account of an incident without checking the facts?

Jesus did not hold the Roman soldiers responsible for their part in his death. He said, "Father, forgive them, for they know not what they do."

PRAYER

Dear Father,
We know that if we had been there, we might well have lacked the
courage needed to stand up for the truth. Help us today to walk
with you into that courtyard, to face our fear, to see what yours
must have been like. We are truly sorry for the times when we have
not questioned sufficiently what we have heard about someone we
know, when we have believed the rumor and, even worse, passed it
on to someone else. Whatever we have done to one of your children
we have done to Jesus. Forgive us, Father. **AMEN.**

Injustice Covered Up

They put a purple robe on Jesus, made a crown out of thorny branches, and put it on his head. Then they began to salute him: "Long live the King of the Jews!" They beat him over the head with a stick, spat on him, fell on their knees, and bowed down to him. MARK 15:17–19

*T*his was the next stage in the sentence of crucifixion. I don't think I'd realized this before. This wasn't something performed especially for Jesus, nor did it stem from a violent hatred. It was quite simply the soldiers' "treat time."

We've seen it before—during the Holocaust, in Cambodia, in Japanese prisoner-of-war camps, in the former Yugoslavia. Doubtless we'll see it again. When given permission to do anything they want and when personal responsibility is removed, people often revert to levels of behavior that are bestial, subhuman. The civilized veneer that society boasts of turns out to be very thin indeed.

Is it significant that these were Roman soldiers, respected, uniformed members of the most successful civilization of the day? It is usually when a country is displaying power most forcibly that it is at its most cruel. Arrogance is dangerous. It separates us in our minds from other people. It offers us the chance to believe that in our superior state we are no longer accountable. Uniforms can have the same effect. At worst, they give the wearer a sense of power that can feel like a license to abuse those of lesser rank. I'm sure we have all had experiences of these minityrants.

Perhaps this is why Jesus chose to live as he did. The example of service he set hardly condones arrogance. At no time in his life did he set himself apart from his followers in terms of lifestyle, dress, or language.

To know that we're accountable to such a God can help to keep us from falling into the trap of indifference to others. No wonder Jesus taught us to pray "Lead us not into temptation." I truly believe that vulnerability is our only safeguard against the temptation to misuse power, whether at work, at home with the family, or even in a situation like that of Jesus and the Roman soldiers.

When they had finished making fun of him, they took off the purple robe and put his own clothes back on him.
MARK 15:20

How I loathe what happened then. Why do I, though? Surely the baying mob and the physical torture of our Savior were much worse. I hate this more because it stinks of a cover-up. My husband, Adrian, once met a social worker who had developed a technique of hitting children with a wet towel in such a way that it left no mark. Presumably, he thought Adrian would find the information useful in his work with disturbed children.

Then there is the friend of ours who was sexually abused over a long period of time, beginning when she was eight years old. Her uncle ensured her silence by threatening that he'd tell her parents she'd led him on. Years later I would hear her sob, "It was all my fault."

"How was it your fault?" I asked—and she told me.

"He said so."

Deeply lodged in this woman's mind is the knowledge of guilt. No adult reasoning can remove those hideous false seeds planted there for her attacker's self-protection and covered over with the soil of secrecy.

When the soldiers replaced Jesus' clothes, covering the jagged, torn flesh of their victim, they were removing the evidence in the same way that we have heard the police removed evidence in the case of the Birmingham Six. The need to cover one's tracks is an admission of guilt and has no place in any viable system of justice. Whatever happened behind the locked doors of a Birmingham police station or in the closed courtyard of the governor's palace is history. But the coldness of purpose involved in the cover-up is as hard for me to forgive as is the silence extorted by my friend's uncle.

࿉

PRAYER

Dear Father,
Help us to hate what you hate and to despise what you despise.
Give us courage to speak out against injustice and bullying and
to tackle those who in any way cause your little ones to stumble.
Teach us how to listen to our conscience more clearly and how to
fine-tune our heartstrings so that we become aware of how you
feel about what is going on around us. Then give us the ability
to respond. AMEN.

Just Being There

Then they led him out to crucify him.   MARK 15:20

⁓ᴐ

The third stage. He's been condemned and beaten, and now the cross is placed across his shoulders and the long walk begins, a showy procession by all accounts. At the head, a centurion carries a placard on which the crime is stated. Four soldiers follow, and in the center, the focus of all attention, walks a man on his way to death. This man had been beaten with a whip made of leather thongs embedded with pieces of metal.

When I was about fourteen, I went hosteling with a youth organization. One blazing afternoon I fell asleep on a grassy bank outside the hostel. The ensuing sunburn kept me awake all night, and the next morning I had to shoulder my backpack and walk seven miles to the next hostel. I will never forget it. My backpack, heavy with sensible wet-weather clothing and clanking with camping kettles, all-in-one cutlery sets, and other useful gadgets, scoured my back every inch of the way.

I thought that was bad, but my small pain was nothing compared to what Jesus suffered. The physical pain he experienced from dragging that unwieldy and immensely heavy burden was compounded by other things, such as the humiliation of being the object of derision and the knowledge, literally impressed on him every inch of the way, that his death lay ahead. I have never been able to rid myself of the memory of those families in Cambodia's killing fields who first had to dig their graves and then had to stand by them waiting to be shot in the back.

Carrying a cross was the same. Not for a second, as he stumbled his way through the city streets and finally out the gates and up the hill, could he be distracted from the reality of what his brief future held.

I don't think our close walk with Jesus is improving, do you?

A large crowd of people followed him; among them were some women who were weeping and wailing for him. LUKE 23:27

I can't help thinking, "Thank goodness for the women." Not that I blame the men. The courage Peter showed in entering that courtyard was enormous, and I don't know a soul who wouldn't have been tempted to deny knowing Jesus when faced with the strong possibility of also being taken prisoner on that confusing and frightening night. The women clearly felt safer. I know that. I'm just so glad they were there, mourning openly for him and making his hideous journey a little less lonely.

Being there usually costs less in terms of time and commitment than picking up the end of someone's cross. But it may cost just as much in terms of bringing judgment upon us. We all like to be part of the crowd. It's safer to agree that so-and-so had it coming to them or to shake our communal head over the way certain people we won't mention are bringing up their children.

I know from personal experience what it's like to be the object of community disapproval. Nothing is more difficult for people to understand than the depression and angry despair that accompany any sort of emotional breakdown. I cannot put into words what it meant to me, when Adrian was ill in this way in 1984, to know that a small handful of people were there for us, openly caring, allowing their support for us to be heard, and never judging us or telling us what we should do.

Yes, I'm so glad the women were there.

PRAYER

Dear Father,
I can't believe that you love us so much that you allowed Jesus to
suffer like this for us. Can we really be worth it? We know people
who are suffering. Help us to walk with them in their desert for as
many blistering miles as it takes. Help us to tend to their wounds,
to help carry their burdens. But above all, help us to never mini-
mize their pain. **AMEN.**

Share the Burden

As they were going, they met a man from Cyrene named Simon who was coming into the city from the country. LUKE 23:26

∽◯

$\mathcal{D}$id you ever have a childhood hero? I did. No, it wasn't a pop singer or an actor. It was this man, Simon of Cyrene. As a child, I went to a Catholic school. Some aspects were rather bizarre to my Protestant mind, but I loved the flowery processions that signified saints' days and, of course, the days off that accompanied them!

One regular aspect of my schooling involved visiting the chapel, where the height of daring (I seem to remember) was squeezing the sponge of holy water dry and flipping our wet hands over our friends. Despite this, I did develop a deep joy at being there. I loved the color, the candles, and the combination of the heavy perfumes of flowers and incense. But most of all I loved the stations of the cross. The one that always drew me to it first was Jesus stumbling under the weight of the cross and falling onto his poor knees. At the age of seven, I didn't understand much about scourging and sacrifice, but I did know all about grazed knees, and I knew how much it hurt when you were carrying something heavy and then crashed with all your weight onto your knees. I remember touching his knees with my finger and the tears that always threatened as I helplessly imagined his pain. Then I would rush to the next station, and there would be this man, Simon, helping him to lift the weight.

Do you, like me, find it rather amusing to imagine what the reaction of some of these "minor" biblical characters would have been if they had discovered how famous they would become? Simon of Cyrene, the hero of a plump little girl in the late twentieth century. What would he have said?

They seized him, put the cross on him, and made him carry it behind Jesus.

Poor Simon, in Jerusalem for the Passover jamboree, all the way from Cyrene in North Africa. Why him? He had probably been saving up his "camel miles" for ages! And now . . . what a way to spend a holiday. On and on, through the streets of Jerusalem, past the jeering crowds, and finally out the city gates. Of course, it wasn't lawful to crucify a man within the boundaries of the city. He knew that. On and on in the searing heat and up the hill Simon stumbled unhappily. What would people think?

Let us stop for a moment and take a breath. Do we know anyone who is at the point of falling under the weight of the cross they are carrying alone? Maybe their cross is illness or depression or a failed relationship or a lost job or bereavement. Often when we look, we discover that someone very close to us is carrying his or her cross alone. Maybe, like Simon, we feel we have been given no choice in helping to carry that burden. Maybe it has hit someone so close to us that we are automatically involved. Maybe we've been asking, "Why me?" and feeling bitter and resentful.

Or perhaps we have a choice. If so, we must think carefully, because each cross will need to be carried to the top of the hill. Having shouldered the burden, it's no good putting it down five yards later. Nor is it any good hoping it will bring glory—it won't. It's no use, either, rushing from person to person picking up crosses and then dropping them to rush off and help someone else.

Cross carrying is never easy, but it is Jesus' way, and it is our chance to walk close to him day by day on the road to Calvary.

⌒෧

MEDITATION

You come to join Jesus. Feel the weight of your cross piercing the skin of your shoulders and scoring your back even deeper than the wounds you received from the soldiers.

Feel the incredible weight of the wood, causing your legs to buckle and tremble.

You stop for a moment, waves of nausea making you sway and stumble on the dusty road.

You try to see where you are, but the blood and sweat dripping through your matted hair blind you.

You try to hear, but the shouting and the sound of horses' hooves prevent you from making out what anyone is saying. You feel as though the end is coming, as though you are going to collapse and die there, on the road. You hear a peculiar rasping noise, and it takes a moment or two for you to realize it is the sound of your own breath.

You are urged forward, but stumble and fall to your knees. You feel strangely distant from yourself, as though you were watching a stranger suffer.

Blackness seeps into your brain. Suddenly you feel the whole cross tip forward as though it were alive, and then you feel the weight lift. You stand shakily.

Someone you can't see is helping you to carry your cross. You move forward slowly, no longer alone.

$$\sim\!\!\partial$$

PRAYER

Dear Father,
Some of us are burdened with a heavy load. Come to us, we beg you. Help us to keep going. Give us just enough strength to carry on. Some of us know someone who is carrying a burden that is far too heavy to carry alone. Give us the courage to pick it up today.
AMEN.

A Way to Help

They took Jesus to a place called Golgotha, which means "The Place of the Skull." There they tried to give him wine mixed with a drug called myrrh, but Jesus would not drink it. Then they crucified him and divided his clothes among themselves, throwing dice to see who would get which piece of clothing. It was nine o'clock in the morning when they crucified him.

MARK 15:22–25

A lot has been said recently about the immunizing effect that so much tragedy on television has had on our emotions. We can only bear so much pain before our defense system kicks in. This usually results in an inability to respond, either in the form of toughened cynicism or a deliberate switching off. For some people, the inability to change the circumstances they see causes impotent despair.

So much has been said and written about the death of Jesus that our response to it can be similarly affected. I know mine has, and as I think about him hanging there, I am engulfed by helplessness. I cannot remove this chapter from his life any more than I, as a little girl staring at those stations of the cross, could heal his poor knees with kisses.

But maybe Jesus has given us a way to enter into his tragedy. If, as Mother Teresa believed, Christ is to be found in every suffering soul, then in them lies our chance to bandage those knees, to ease the weight from those bleeding shoulders, and to be there for him at the end. It is a glorious opportunity. Let's take it.

<u>PRAYER</u>

Dear Father,
Thank you for the many opportunities we have to help our suffer-
ing world. Help us to find the right way to make a difference and
to seize the opportunity at whatever cost to ourselves. **AMEN.**

When Hope Is Gone

Standing close to Jesus' cross were his mother, his mother's sister, Mary the wife of Clopas, and Mary Magdalene. Jesus saw his mother and the disciple he loved standing there; so he said to his mother, "He is your son."

Then he said to the disciple, "She is your mother." From that time the disciple took her to live in his home.

Jesus knew that by now everything had been completed....

Then he bowed his head and gave up his spirit....

After this, Joseph, who was from the town of Arimathea, asked Pilate if he could take Jesus' body. (Joseph was a follower of Jesus, but in secret, because he was afraid of the Jewish authorities.) Pilate told him he could have the body, so Joseph went and took it away.   JOHN 19:25–28, 30, 38

You were there, standing with the other women close to the cross, loyal to the very end. How did you feel, looking at your dear firstborn son hanging there, beaten, bruised, humiliated? Did you wonder about the truth of the prophecy you had received? "He will cause the mighty to fall"? It didn't seem too possible then. Simeon's sword piercing your side was far more accurate.

Did you remember his birth, the shepherds, the kings? His first toddling steps, his first words? Oh Mary, how did you feel?

Did you feel that you had failed? That if you had been able to stem the rushing tide he would be safe now? Did you chide yourself for not having seen the signs earlier? Did you wish that Joseph was by your side so you could lean on him? Did you try to be strong for your dying son or did you weep helplessly in your sister's arms?

How was it having Mary Magdalene there? Were you friends, or did she represent the lifestyle that had brought your son to this appalling end? We will never know. All we know is that you were there, with the women. As Anne from Jane Austen's *Persuasion* says, "All the privilege I claim for my own sex is that of loving longest when existence or when hope is gone."

The role of parents throughout the ages has been to be there when their children are going through the worst of times. It is often all we can do. When Adrian and I were working with at-risk children we saw so many of them with large gaping holes inside them that should have been filled with memories of being loved. That's what we can do for our children during their childhood years. We may make all the mistakes in the world, but if we have stuffed them full of love, we haven't completely failed.

Then we have to let them go, a painful, ripping gesture that we probably never quite come to terms with. We have to stand in the wings of their lives, mouthing our support, sometimes having to swallow our jealousy or our criticism of their performance and of those to whom they have given leading roles in their lives. Then and only then have we earned the right to stand there in the worst times, to be there at the cross. Thank you, Mary. You stand in my eyes for the very best of parenting.

PRAYER

Dear Father,
Thank you for the example of the woman you chose to be the
mother of your Son. You certainly knew what you were doing. Help
us to learn from her how to be there for those whom we love, what-
ever the cost.   AMEN.

Alive for Ever and Ever!

After the Sabbath, at dawn on the first day of the week, Mary Magdalene and the other Mary went to look at the tomb.

There was a violent earthquake, for an angel of the Lord came down from heaven and, going to the tomb, rolled back the stone and sat on it. His appearance was like lightning, and his clothes were white as snow. The guards were so afraid of him that they shook and became like dead men.

The angel said to the women, "Do not be afraid, for I know that you are looking for Jesus, who was crucified. He is not here; he has risen, just as he said. Come and see the place where he lay. Then go quickly and tell his disciples: 'He has risen from the dead and is going ahead of you into Galilee. There you will see him.' Now I have told you."

So the women hurried away from the tomb, afraid yet filled with joy, and ran to tell his disciples. Suddenly Jesus met them. "Greetings," he said. They came to him, clasped his feet and worshiped him. Then Jesus said to them, "Do not be afraid. Go and tell my brothers to go to Galilee; there they will see me."

MATTHEW 28:1–10 (NIV)

∽◯

*T*his day is one of the most glorious muddles in the whole of the New Testament. You'd think that accounts of this day of all days would have tallied. Yet all the Gospel writers have a differ-ent tale, a different emphasis. In different accounts, we read about stones rolling back (or no stone at all), an angel (or two), several women who pass on the good news (or don't), and a whole lot of disciples who believe that Jesus has risen (or don't).

Wouldn't it have made sense to stick to one story line, God? But what these variations show is that everyone wanted to be part of the Resurrection, and I'm sure that everyone knew someone who knew someone who had been there. The wonderful truth shared by them all is that Jesus came back to life. But when we consider this glorious truth, we must see it in its full context. Mary Magdalene would have her precious memories—and I so love Jesus for singling out one of his favorite cracked pots for special attention. Peter and John would have their own stories. Even the Roman soldiers would have a tale to tell.

But we are the most fortunate because we have all the accounts. We have the hindsight of Peter at the time of Pentecost, and we have the amazing revelation to John that the one who came back is in fact the risen Lord in all his glory.

I turned around to see the voice that was speaking to me. And when I turned I saw seven golden lampstands, and among the lampstands was someone "like a son of man," dressed in a robe reaching down to his feet and with a golden sash around his chest. His head and hair were white like wool, as white as snow, and his eyes were like blazing fire. His feet were like bronze glowing in a furnace, and his voice was like the sound of rushing waters. In his right hand he held seven stars, and out of his mouth came a sharp double-edged sword. His face was like the sun shining in all its brilliance.

When I saw him, I fell at his feet as though dead. Then he placed his right hand on me and said: "Do not be afraid. I am the First and the Last. I am the Living One; I was dead, and behold I am alive for ever and ever! And I hold the keys of death and Hades." REVELATION 1:12–18 (NIV)

To me this is the best truth of all. It is he, all-powerful, who stands and knocks at the door of our heart, he who wants to come into the house of our life and eat with us and we with him. The risen Lord of glory, whose face shines like the sun. The Holy One of God, our creator and our dearest friend.

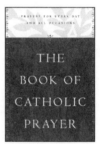
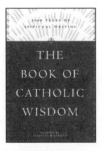